SHOW ME THE GREEN!

WRITTEN BY
D.S. VENETTA

Show Me the Green!
Wild Tales & Garden Thrills

Show Me The Green! ~ Book #1
Beans, Greens & Grades ~ Book #2

Book #3 will explore community &
library gardens ~ spring 2017

Coloring books for each title are available featuring all of
the illustrations from the book ~ perfect for engaging
younger children in the adventure of gardening!

Talula—

SHOW ME THE GREEN!

Enjoy the adventure!

Benedetta

ISBN: 978-0-9911182-9-8
Publisher: BloominThyme Press
Editor: Best Foot Forward
Illustrations by MikeMotz.com
Copyright © 2015 D.S. Venetta

Publisher's Cataloging-In-Publication Data
(Prepared by The Donohue Group, Inc.)

Names: Venetta, D. S. | MikeMotz.com, illustrator.
Title: Show me the green! / written by D.S. Venetta ; illustrations by MikeMotz.com.
Description: [Leesburg, Florida] : BloominThyme Press, [2015] | Series: Wild tales & garden thrills ; book 1 | Interest age level: 007-009. | Summary: A brother and sister sign on to win a farmer's market contest and work to grow organic vegetables in their backyard. The story follows the siblings from planting seeds to harvest, teaching readers the basic tenets of organic gardening as well as exposing them to the wildlife, bugs, and other fun things to be found.
Identifiers: ISBN 978-0-9911182-9-8 (print) | ISBN 978-1-5168-0152-7 (print) | ISBN 978-0-9964391-0-7 (ebook)
Subjects: LCSH: Organic gardening--Juvenile fiction. | Brothers and sisters--Juvenile fiction. | Contests--Juvenile fiction. CYAC: Organic gardening--Fiction. | Brothers and sisters--Fiction. | Contests--Fiction.
Classification: LCC PZ7.1.V46 Sh 2015 (print) | LCC PZ7.1.V46 (ebook) | DDC [Fic]--dc23

*This book is dedicated to my children.
It was their assistance and enthusiasm in the
early days of my gardening career that truly
ignited my passion, paving the way for my
school garden adventures, my blog, and beyond.
They are the best!*

ACKNOWLEDGEMENTS

For several years, I volunteered in my children's school garden where there was never a dull moment to be had between the beds of fruits and vegetables. How could there be? As every gardener knows, there are simply too many exciting things to be found among the leaves and in the dirt, hovering about the blossoms and soaring in the sky, waiting for you to leave. Gardening is about more than growing a bunch of plants—it's about discovering our relationship with nature, the cycle of life that continues around us, how we fit in, and how we're interconnected. It's amazing once you stop and really take a look. And from what I've learned, kids are some of the best observers.

It was from those observations that I derived the inspiration for this book. At first, my thoughts took the form of blog posts on my website, BloominThyme, where I shared our weekly garden visits and experiences. However, it wasn't long before characters started popping into my head with adventures and observations of their own! (I'm a writer and that's how our brains work.) Of course, I had to get these musings out of my mind and onto paper and from there, a book was born.

This process took some time to complete. Ideas flow quickly and easily, but the words and storyline required development. A huge thank you goes to three young ladies who helped enormously in this regard via their editorial comments. Hailey, Riley, and Cassidy Reale took the time to read my novel and offer their brilliant insight and middle grade wisdom. I couldn't have done it without them! Another big thank you goes to Mrs. Grier, Mrs. Thompson and their students. From Lake Montessori to Lake Preparatory, these kids not only worked in the school garden with me, but they returned valuable feedback once chapters were written, helping me to get it right and keep it interesting.

I hope readers will enjoy reading *Show Me the Green!* as much as I've enjoyed writing it. It's certainly been an adventure...

TABLE OF CONTENTS

SHOW ME THE GREEN!

1

FARMER'S MARKET

Lexi Williams tapped her foot impatiently as her mom inspected a big round head of cabbage. She squeezed, sniffed, and tapped it twice. It was her usual ritual at the local outdoor market. "That's gross."

Her brother, Jason, rolled his eyes. "I know. Who wants to eat that cabbage after she's put her hands all over it?" Holding a frosty lemonade, he gulped down a swallow. "She always tells *me* to keep my hands off everything and look at her."

Lexi glanced around, taking a sip of

her lemonade slush. The only reason she liked to come to the Farmer's Market was for the fruity slushes. You could buy vegetables at the grocery store but you couldn't get these yummy drinks. Swirling a straw through the yellow liquid, Lexi breathed in the scent of it with a sigh. This was almost as good as dessert!

Jason elbowed her arm. "Hey, look—"

"Ouch!" Lexi glared at him. "What did you do that for?"

"We can win tickets to the Fall Festival," he said, and pointed to a poster pinned on a post. Her father was leaning against it, relaxed, while holding their younger brother, Timmy. "And a hundred dollars!"

Tickets to the festival? Lexi zeroed in on the green and white sign. Quickly, she read. *First Annual Kids' Gardening Contest. Win two tickets to the County Fall Festival and $100 prize money for the best produce.*

"I wonder what you have to do." She looked to Jason. "Grow stuff?"

"I don't know, but I wanna win a hundred dollars! Then I could buy those sneakers for soccer that Mom says are too expensive. Let's go ask!" he said, and took off running without waiting for a reply.

Reason number one hundred forty-seven not to like brothers: *They're selfish and self-serving.* Still, Lexi hurried over just in time to hear Jason begging, "Can we enter, Mom? Please? Can we? I really want to win!"

Mom smiled. She smiled and placed a hand on Jason's shoulder. "Well, sure we can, but I didn't think you enjoyed the garden all that much last summer."

"Gardening?" Lexi quipped. "Jason doesn't care about gardening—he only wants the hundred dollars!"

Mom raised her brow and Jason shot Lexi the "look" before answering, "That's not true! Well—it is," he corrected quickly, "I do want the money, but I liked gardening okay."

"You did not," Lexi said, refusing to be drawn in by his sad, puppy-dog face.

"Did so."

Lexi crossed her arms over her chest. "And what if I want to win the money?"

"You can have the tickets," he said. "You like going to the festival, anyway."

"And you don't?"

Chuckling, Mom raised a hand. "That's enough. I think it's a great idea, and I'd say you two have a real chance at winning."

"Winning what?" Dad asked as he walked over, Timmy skipping behind him like any normal five-year-old.

"A garden contest," Mom replied, and pointed to the poster.

Dad read the details while Timmy tried to pull the cabbage from his hands. He let out a low whistle. "A hundred dollars?

That's a lot of cabbage!" He laughed, as though he'd made a joke.

"Yes," Jason blurted. "I want the money and Lexi can have the tickets."

"What if I want the money?" Lexi repeated.

"How about you both garden, you both share?" Dad offered. "We have a big backyard. There should be plenty enough room for both of you."

Lexi and Jason locked gazes. There was no way she was going to share her tickets with Jason. She wanted to invite her best friend Amy Atkins to the fair. Last year Amy had gone with Kimberly Evans, and she'd been hogging her friend's attention ever since. A flicker of desire trickled into Lexi's heart as she imagined her and Amy at the fair, having the best time in the world. Kimberly would be so jealous when Amy went with Lexi—and for free! When word got around,

she'd be the most popular girl in school.

"Fine," Lexi said to Jason, whipping her slushy to one side. "You can have the money but *I* get the tickets."

He grinned. "Awesome."

"Aren't you two forgetting something?" Mom asked.

They turned and asked at the same time, "What?"

"You haven't won yet. First, we have to make a plan and decide what to grow."

"I wanna grow potatoes!" Jason called out.

"I love potatoes!" Timmy said, clasping his hands together.

"I'm growing carrots," Lexi said. They were easy, and it was fun to cut their green "hair" as they sprouted.

"How about we go home and draw up a plan?" Glancing back at the poster, Mom added, "We'd better hurry. Judging begins in early September."

Jason frowned. "Not until then?"

Mom laughed. "It's already middle of May! Your vegetables will need that time to grow."

When they arrived home, Dad took Timmy outside to play while Lexi and Jason joined Mom at the kitchen table. It was time to decide who was going to grow what. "I call carrots," Lexi said.

"I call potatoes," Jason shot back.

Mom started making notes on a yellow pad of paper. "Okay. What else?"

"What else?" Jason's mouth hung open. "How much do we have to grow?"

"I suggest you each pick two and I'll pick a few."

"But the contest is for kids, Mom. You can't enter."

"No." She winked. "But I can still grow vegetables. I loved our garden last year." Writing down the words as she said them, Mom continued, "I'll grow green beans, tomatoes, broccoli, and beets. And corn for Dad."

"Corn for Dad?" Jason asked.

"He loves corn with his burgers. Besides, that's the first rule of gardening..."

"What rule?"

"Grow what you'll eat."

Lexi balked. Did that mean she had to eat all the carrots? There was no way. And if she didn't, what would happen to them? She remembered all too well the cucumbers that rotted on the vine last year because nobody wanted to eat them. *Ick*. Lexi had only picked carrots because she could use some to make carrot cake with her mom.

"Okay," Jason said. "Then I'll grow red beans, too."

Mom wrote it down. "For your chili."

Jason beamed. "Yep!"

"Okay," she replied. "I have potatoes

and beans for Jason. Carrots and…?" Mom looked to Lexi. "What else would you like to grow?"

"Can I grow sweet potatoes?" Lexi asked. She loved sweet potatoes, when served in the form of a pie!

"You bet you can," Mom said. "The second rule of gardening is knowing when your plants will grow. Sweet potatoes like warm weather so summer is the perfect time for them. But you'll need to get your slips started as soon as possible. Sweet potatoes take almost four months to grow."

Lexi smiled, feeling the first wave of excitement. Making sweet potato slips was fun. Before you could grow them, you had to sprout them. First, she had to cut a sweet potato in half, then poke it with toothpicks. That was so she could perch it over a glass full of water. Then, when she put it in a sunny window, the potato would start to sprout—which was cool!

"Next up," Mom said, "we have to till the dirt in our old garden and form new beds."

Jason brightened. "You mean loosen the dirt, because plants like their beds soft and fluffy."

Mom smiled and gave a light pinch to Jason's cheek. "That's right—you remembered!"

Lexi glowered. *Showoff.* "Why do we call rows of dirt 'beds,' anyway?"

Mom peered at Lexi. "I'm not sure."

"And why can't we use the old ones?" Jason asked. "Wouldn't that mean less work?"

Mom smiled. "It would, but after a year of sun and rain, the soil will be too hard and our plants won't be able to absorb nutrients from the soil."

"Nutrients?" Jason asked.

"Food," Lexi snapped.

"Lexi's right. Nutrients is another word for plant food. Like the vitamins you need to stay healthy, plants need nutrients."

"Oh." Jason lifted his brow. "Can I use the shovel?"

"Yes," Mom replied, and setting down her pen.

"Can I rake them?" Lexi asked. This was her garden, too. No reason her brother should get to use all the garden tools.

"Of course you can." Mom flipped a paper over her pad and started a new page. "Let's make a list of things we need. And this year, let's keep a journal. It will make it easy to keep track of our progress."

"So we can win money," Jason said.

"So we can win tickets," Lexi corrected.

"So we can keep organized," Mom said. "September will be here before you know it."

2

FLASHY WHEELS

Later that afternoon, Jason, Lexi, Timmy, and Mom headed to the hardware store for supplies. Peering into their cart, they could see it was full of some pretty boring stuff—gardening gloves for Lexi, packets of seeds, plant food. Jason had only agreed to come along because he figured he should be here to help with the heavy lifting and stuff. But so far the heaviest thing they'd had to lift was a five-pound bag of all-natural fertilizer. As they turned down the next aisle, he spotted a shiny red

wagon parked at the other end. He bolted for it.

"Jason!" his mom called after him. "We don't run through the store!"

Reaching the wagon, he grabbed the black handle and whirled around. "Mom, I *need* this!"

Lexi snorted and marched down the aisle, her black ponytail swinging behind her. "You don't *need* that wagon—you *want* it. There's a difference."

Jason scowled. "Keep out of it."

Mom and Timmy caught up with them and Jason begged, "*Please*, Mom. It will make our job in the garden so much easier. Think of all the vegetables I can carry with this thing!"

Timmy hopped into the wagon.

"It will help *you*, too, Mom," Jason added eagerly. "You won't have to carry your garden bag anymore. You could roll it!"

"You make good points," Mom replied, lifting Timmy free from the wagon, telling him, "No, that's not for climbing." She glanced between Jason and Lexi and paused. "Jason's right. It will make our job a lot easier. Especially harvesting."

Jason beamed.

Mom brought a finger to her mouth and peered at Lexi. "You might need a new pair of clippers."

"For what?"

"Your carrots, remember?"

Lexi's mood bounced back. "Yes—for their haircut!"

"And Jason, didn't you tell me you wanted to help build the trellis?"

Jason perked up. A trellis? Kinda like a fence for plants to climb as they grew, a trellis would be fun to build. But he'd need supplies. "Are we doing that today?"

"We can," Mom offered.

"Awesome! I'll need some wood, nails,

and a saw." He paused as a thought struck. "Dad can help me with the sawing."

"Don't forget about the twine," his mom reminded him.

"Twine?"

"Yes. We'll use it to support my beans as they grow."

"Your trellis had better be strong," Lexi said. "Last year our beans fell all over the ground because the sticks we used to hold them weren't big enough."

"My trellis is going to be plenty strong," Jason said, pulling himself up to his full height—which was still about a foot shorter than Lexi. And he was glad to help his mom. After all, it was a man's job to build things. "You can grow all the beans you want, Mom. I've got you covered."

"Thanks, honey." She placed a hand on his shoulder. "I'm sure it will be great."

"Can I paint it?" Lexi asked. "It should

be pretty."

Mom smiled. "Yes. You're right. It should be pretty." She lowered herself to Timmy's level and took his hands in hers. "But no climbing on it, okay? It's for beans only."

"Okay!" Timmy clapped. "Can I help build it?"

Jason shot him a wary gaze.

"Jason?" Mom prodded.

"I guess..." he muttered. "But I'm in charge."

When they returned home, Mom and Lexi retreated to the garden shed to prepare for the tilling while Dad gathered his tools from the work shed.

Up at the house, Jason said, "Hop in, Timmy. I'll give you a ride to the garden."

"Okay!" Timmy said. He quickly climbed aboard the wagon and said, "Let's go!"

"Hold on," Jason told him. "We're gonna go fast!"

Timmy clenched the sides with all his might. "Okay. I like to go *fast*."

Jason grinned. "Here we go!"

Timmy held tight as the wagon bumped over the gently sloped lawn. "Wheeeeee!"

As they traveled, the wagon began to accelerate on its own.

"Faster! Faster!" Timmy cheered.

Jason ran even faster as the hill steepened.

Too fast—they were rapidly approaching the forest of trees behind their backyard. *Uh*-oh. He swerved to avoid a pile of bamboo stakes set out for Mom's green beans, but the wagon side-swiped them with a thud. Skinny sticks went flying into the air. Jason shot a look back at his brother. Amazingly, Timmy still held strong.

"Jason!" Dad shouted. "Stop that right now!"

He wanted to stop, but they were going too fast. Just then, the toe of his sneaker caught in a ditch and he tripped, slamming to the ground. The wagon smashed into his back. *OUCH* *That would leave a bruise.*

Turning, he asked, "You okay, Timmy?"

The kid nodded, still clutching the sides of the wagon as if they weren't finished. But they were. Mom rushed over, frantic. Yep, they were definitely *finished.*

"Are you boys all right?"

Jason peered up at his mom, the anger in her eyes unmistakable. Maybe he should cry. The sympathy card might work right about now. At least it would soften the blow. "The wagon smashed into me," Jason said, rubbing his back with an exaggerated wince. "I might have crushed some bones."

"What were you thinking, Jason? You know better than that!"

He started to apologize, but Timmy let out a war whoop. "Can we do it again?" his brother asked Mom. "Can we?"

Jason smiled but quickly wiped the expression off his face when he saw his dad walking up to them. Time for the real hammer to come down.

"I don't ever want to see another child in that wagon again," Dad scolded. "Do you understand?"

Jason looked at the ground. "Yes, sir."

"The wagon is for plants, not people."

"Yes, sir." Jason's back was beginning to throb. His head was beginning to ache, but he didn't dare complain about either one.

"Are you okay?" Dad asked.

Jason knew better than to try to milk his dad for sympathy. "I think I just bruised it."

"Glad to hear it. We have work to do, but you are officially on yard duty tomorrow—all day."

"Yes, sir," Jason said again, getting to his feet. He wasn't nearly as excited about building the trellis as he had been just a few minutes ago. When Dad was in a "mood," building became work, not fun. But at least he didn't seem *too* angry with him over the wipeout.

Jason and Dad cut wood into five-foot lengths while Mom, Lexi, and Timmy outlined the new beds that needed to be formed. Dad stretched his measuring tape along a piece of wood and held it there. "I think a foot deep will be strong enough to keep the trellis in place," he said, looking to Mom. "Wouldn't you agree?"

"Yes. A foot should be plenty. When they're finished, run them down this row, please? And this row." Mom indicated the two rows closest to her. "Our beans will be located here."

Lexi pointed toward the opposite end of the garden. "But weren't the beans over there last year?"

"Yes, but remember, we need to change their position each year."

"Why? Wouldn't it be easier to just keep them in the same place?"

"Easier, yes," Mom agreed. "But not better. If you plant the same plant in the same place year after year, the bugs will know exactly where to find it and they will eat it up before it has a chance to grow!"

"Seriously?" Lexi scoffed. Was she making this stuff up? Sometimes Mom did that—just made up stories as she went along. Except when Lexi tried it, Mom called it telling tales. *Parents*. Go figure.

"Yes, seriously," Mom said. "Crop rotation is one of the keys to successful or-

ganic gardening. We change the plant location each year because it's better for the plant. Besides bugs, we also change plant locations because some plants are heavy feeders," Mom continued, "and clean the soil."

"Plants don't actually clean the soil," Lexi replied, but hesitated. *"Do they?"*

Her mom laughed. "When I say they 'clean' the soil, I mean they remove all the nutrients. Take corn, for instance. That plant will use up every bit of food in the soil it possibly can!"

Lexi grinned. "Probably why corn on the cob tastes so good."

Mom nodded. "And healthy. Tomatoes are heavy feeders, too. Beans, on the other hand, actually put nutrients back into the soil. So this year, we'll plant beans where we planted our tomatoes last year. Remember our song?"

Lexi chimed in immediately, "Beans-leaves-roots-and-fruits! Beans feed, leaves need, roots move in, and fruits take out!"

Mom laughed. "That's right! You remembered."

How could she forget? Last summer Lexi couldn't get the jingle out of her head. It was supposed to help her keep track of which plants needed what. Angling her head, she thought happily, *guess it worked!*

"That's smart gardening," Dad observed.

"That's gardening with Mother Nature."

"But how are we going to keep track of it all?" Lexi asked.

"Keep a journal. Let's sketch a diagram of the garden and color code the plant families."

"Can I color it in?"

"What?"

"The journal."

Mom smiled. "You bet. But first, we need to get digging. We need to scoop the dirt, then rake it smooth."

"Hey," Jason called out and frowned. "I thought I was using the shovel."

Mom looked at the saw in his hand and said, "But you're busy building the trellis. Would you rather dig or saw?"

Jason glanced at the garden then down at the saw in hand, then back to the garden. His expression fell. "I guess I'll saw."

"Fine. Lexi and I will till the garden while you and Dad build the trellis."

"Can you dig and I rake?" Lexi asked.

"Sure," Mom said. "And remember, we need to pull any weeds we see along the way." She turned to Timmy. "Can you grab them as we work our way down each row?"

Timmy nodded. "Okay."

The two went straight to work, scooping dirt up, moving it over, raking it smooth. Up, over, rake it smooth. Up, over, rake it smooth. After an hour, Lexi stood and surveyed their handiwork. Row after row was straight and even, with smoothly raked flat tops. "Wow. It looks almost too nice to mess up with plants."

Jason walked over and stood beside her. "Are we ready to plant?"

"Not yet," Mom said. "First we need to add compost to the soil." She glanced over her shoulder. "Are you ready to put up your trellis?"

He checked with Dad who nodded. Jason grinned. "Yep!"

"Great," Mom replied. "If you two will place it down there," she pointed to the old tomato row, "Lexi and I will go get the wagon and load up the compost."

Pulling the wagon over to their outdoor compost pile, a big mess of rotting food and leaves, Lexi helped Mom shovel the inky black compost-dirt into the wag-

on. Timmy followed, but Mom wouldn't let him touch anything. "That's not for play," she said. "That's for the plants."

"But I want to help," he protested.

Mom paused, then walked into the garden shed and came out with a shiny object in her hand. "How about I put you in charge of the wind chime?"

Timmy's eyes lit up. "Okay," he replied, and took the colorful frog-shaped figure from her.

When the wagon was full, Lexi pulled it to the garden and started dumping compost down the middle of each row. When they finished, Lexi ditched the shovel and grabbed the rake.

Jason darted over and said, "Hey, I wanted to help with the rake."

"You're building the trellis."

Jason tossed a thumb over his shoulder. "Dad's got it."

Lexi eyed the dirt then her brother.

Raking was the fun part. It's when she got to make everything look nice and neat. Jason stuck out his hand. Mom peered between them. "Fine," she said, and handed over the rake. Whirling, she went to the picnic table and grabbed her drawing pad and markers. *She* was in charge of the journal. Finding a soft spot of grass off to one side, Lexi sat cross-legged and watched as Mom and Timmy hung the wind chime from an oversized hook.

"This should keep the birds away," Mom declared.

"You think birds are going to be afraid of a fake frog?" Lexi asked.

Admiring her handiwork, Mom lifted Timmy up so that he could touch it as it twirled. "They're afraid of its shiny surface. When it turns in the breeze, it reflects sharp bursts of sunlight that startle the birds."

"Oh." *Dumb birds*, Lexi thought and

flipped her pad open. At least the frog had lots of purple, which meant it would be pretty to draw.

Day One in the Garden...

We started our garden to win the Farmer's Market contest. First, we had to go to the store and buy tools and gloves. Jason almost broke the new wagon we bought to help with the garden but luckily, it's okay. (And really helpful to carry the heavy stuff.) Jason worked on the trellis with Dad while I helped Mom make the rows. We had to loosen the dirt really well, because plants like their beds soft and fluffy.

I'm planting carrots and sweet potatoes. Jason is planting potatoes and kidney beans. Mom is planting corn, tomatoes, beets, and green beans. We're putting stuff in different places than last year to trick the bugs. (I can't believe they wait and hide in the soil for a whole year just to eat our vegetables!) That's about it. So far, so good.

P.S. I'm coloring the journal so it will look pretty.

3

SLIPPERY EGGS & SEEDS

Sitting three rows over from his mom, Jason opened a brown bag. Now that he'd made his holes, it was time to start planting potato seeds. They weren't actually seeds, but small red-skinned potatoes. Staring into the bag of almost ten of them, he blew out a heavy sigh. Why did they buy so many? Each one had to be cut in half which would double the amount of work! His friend, Nathan Lampert, was supposed to come over later, but now it looked like he'd be here planting these things all day. He also had beans to plant. *Ugh*. Why did he agree to this garden, again?

An image of neon green cleats with a black shoe company logo popped into his brain. *Soccer shoes*, he reminded himself. *Soccer shoes. And totally worth it.* Taking a deep breath, he reached for the first potato.

"Do you remember how to plant them?" Mom asked.

"Yes. We cut them in half, and then set them in the hole, skin-side up."

"That's right." She pulled a potato from the bag and held it beside his. "Do you remember what these are called?"

Duh, he wanted to reply, but didn't. "Eyes," he said.

"Correct. Each half you cut must have 'eyes' on it."

Looking at the tiny nubs of sprouts on the potato skin, he knew each little dot was actually a sprout ready to grow. If he planted a piece with no "eye," no new potato would grow. Which meant no prize potatoes. No prize potatoes meant no prize money. No prize money meant no new soccer cleats. Jason took the potato from her. "Can I have the knife?"

"Promise to be careful with it?"

"Yes."

"Okay." His mom handed him the kitchen knife and said, "Set the potato on the ground to cut it. And be careful—you don't want to cut off your finger."

Jason doubted the knife his mom used to spread peanut butter on his sandwiches was going to cut off his finger, but nodded anyway. She was weird that way, always warning him about something that was totally safe. Placing the potato on the ground, he inspected both sides to be sure there were sprout eyes, and then cut it right down the middle. Actually, he had to

saw it down the middle, the knife blade was so dull.

When half of the potato rolled free, his mom exclaimed, "Good job!"

He rolled his eyes. "*Mo*-m…"

Smiling, she checked the row of dirt beside him and said, "Your holes look good and deep. Skin side up, right?" Mom gave him a thumb up. "That way your sprouts can shoot straight up and out of the soil."

"Can you help?" he asked.

"Maybe when I finish with the corn."

"Okay."

Watching his mom return to her row, he knew he'd been chancing it, but it was worth a try. She kneeled down and started dropping corn kernel after corn kernel into a neat row of slightly raised holes she'd made across the top of the dirt. Crawling on hands and knees down her row, she continued her planting.

Jason watched for a minute longer then dropped his potato halves into two holes, and reached for the next one.

"Well, what do we have here?"

Jason glanced over at his mom as she reached into the dirt and pulled something free. Sitting back on her heels, she held up the small white oval and inspected it closely, turning it back and forth between her gloved fingers. "What do you think it is?"

Jason sprang up. Ditching the bag of potatoes, he leapt over his row and the next as he ran to his mother.

"Don't step on the beds!" she exclaimed.

He cleared them with room to spare and landed next to her. "Let me have that!"

She frowned. "*May* I have that please," she corrected.

This was no time for manners—did she not understand what she was holding in her hand? But realizing he would get nowhere fast, Jason rattled off, "*May* I have that please." Then he stuck out his hand.

She handed it over.

Careful not to destroy the find, Jason gently turned it over in his hands and examined it with an experienced eye. "Do you know what this is?" It was more statement than question.

"No," she replied. "I asked you first, remember?"

"This, is a lizard egg," he declared, as though announcing a king's arrival then held it up between forefinger and thumb for her to see.

"A lizard egg?" She peered at it with more interest.

Fearful she might try and snag it from him—now that she knew how valuable a find it was—Jason pulled it out of her reach.

"Are you sure?" she asked.

He nodded. "Very. I learned about these when I found one with Nathan. We saw the baby lizard actually pop right out of it!"

"Wow."

Placing the egg in the palm of his hand, he cupped his other hand over the egg, and leaned over the hole where she'd been digging. "Where did you find it?" He scanned the area and saw nothing but black dirt and open holes filled with pale yellow corn kernels. "Are there any more?"

She looked down at her bed of dirt and shook her head. "No. It's the only one."

"We need some dirt."

"Dirt?" Mom laughed and extended her arms outward. "Great, get some—it's all around you!"

"I need dirt to hatch it, but not here in

the garden."

"You don't think it can hatch out here by itself?"

Jason stared at her. Mothers didn't understand *anything* about nature. This wasn't a potato he could simply cover with dirt and expect to grow. No. This was a living creature that needed a special habitat—one *he* would have to construct.

But it wasn't her fault. She was a *girl* after all. "I need extra dirt so I can hatch this egg. It needs protection. I mean, do you know how many animals like to eat lizard eggs? Snakes, birds..." Jason glanced about the area. "Why, they're probably watching us right now, hiding in bushes as we speak."

His mom smiled and for a second, Jason thought she was going to laugh. "But if you take it away from the garden, honey, it won't be able to eat the insects that will soon try to eat our plants."

He gaped at his mother. Is that all she thought about? The plants? "Mom," he said, using his best stern tone, the one that let others know he meant business. "I need to find a box and I need some dirt. That way I can be sure he survives."

His mom said nothing. She only looked at him, then at his egg and back at him.

While Jason waited, his skin grew warm. Beads of sweat popped across his forehead. If she tried to stop him, he didn't have a plan. What if she insisted he leave the egg here? What if she refused logic and forced him to sacrifice the baby lizard? What if she chose the plant life over the life of this animal?

Caught in the middle of a standoff, Jason needed an alternative. His gaze drifted about the garden. What was he going to do? He willed an answer to appear in his brain and blurted, "You can always get a frog. They like to eat bugs."

Mom frowned. "Frogs need a wet habitat to be happy. They won't be able to survive out here."

Tightening his hold over the egg, Jason drew cupped hands snug against his body. "Leave the sprinkler on."

"Not an option." Mom eyed the egg within his grip. "But I'll let you keep that one."

Yes!

"On one condition."

No...

"You must promise me you'll return the lizard to the garden when he hatches. I need that little guy on insect duty."

"Promise," Jason snapped and turned on his heel. He raced toward the house—fuming mad over the promise his mother just forced out of him. It was *his* lizard! Why should he have to return it to the garden? She didn't need it to eat any in-

sects—she had bug-killing spray for that!

In his hurry to protect his lizard egg—and figure a way out of his promise—Jason nearly ran over his sister.

"Hey, watch where you're going!" Lexi shouted.

"You ran into me!" he hollered back at her on the way to his room.

Lexi yelled at the back of his sandy brown head, "I did not! You ran into *me*!" Reason number two hundred and thirty-nine not to like brothers: *They're rude and careless.*

Continuing down to the garden with her packet of carrot seeds, Lexi announced, "Jason ran into me and almost knocked me over."

"I'm sorry about your brother," Mom replied. "He's in a hurry to save his lizard egg."

"Lizard egg?"

"Yes." Her mom swiped the back of a

gloved hand against her brow. "I found one while planting my corn."

"*And you let him have it?*" Was her mother crazy? Jason didn't know anything about lizards—except about torturing them as he plucked the tails from their yucky, wriggly, scaly little bodies.

"He promised to return it to the garden once it's hatched."

"Don't count on it," Lexi mumbled under her breath. "I'm going to plant my carrots."

"Wonderful."

"Which row is it again?"

"The one where we planted the cabbage last year."

Beans-leaves-roots-and-fruits. Carrots were considered a root, growing underground. Cabbage were leaves—an easy one to remember, since they were all leaves. "Okay." Lexi nodded. That made sense. And her garden had to make sense or she wouldn't win those tickets to the festival. She'd already told Amy about it and her friend was thrilled. *Go to the fair with you? For free? Of course!*

Warm feelings rushed into Lexi. Amy had said *yes*. She was going to the festival with her and not with Kimberly Evans. But first things first—she had to plant her carrots.

"Do you want me to help you?" Mom asked.

"No. I think I remember how to do it."

Kneeling, Lexi began at one end of her row and drew the tip of her forefinger down the top of the dirt, careful not to press too hard. Carrot seeds were teeny-tiny and needed to be planted shallow. If they were too deep, the sprouts would never make it to the surface.

Lexi then pinched a bunch of carrot seeds between her forefinger and thumb,

and sprinkled them down the groove. Since there were so many seeds and she couldn't keep them far enough apart, the sprouts would be too close together. That's when she'd give them a haircut. *The fun part!*

After Lexi ran out of seeds, she carefully covered them with dirt. Pushing up from the ground, she walked over to her mom. "All finished."

"Aren't you going to water them?"

Lexi slumped. "Oh, yeah. I forgot." She walked over to the hose and turned it on, spraying her newly planted seeds with a light mist. If she watered them too heavily, the seeds would float to the surface and she'd have to start all over again.

"Have you started your sweet potato sprouts yet?"

"Yep. Dad helped me while you and Jason were down here."

"Wonderful!"

The mention of her brother kicked her memory into action. "Isn't Jason supposed to be planting his potatoes?"

"He will." Her mom turned toward the house.

"He'd better or we're not going to win the contest!"

Mom smiled. "Don't worry, honey. Your brother won't let you down. He wants to win as much as you do."

Hmph. Lexi planted a hand to her hip and said, "I'll bet he's up there playing with that lizard egg and forgot all about his potatoes."

Her mom sighed. "You don't know that, Lexi."

I know my brother, she thought, but kept her lips zipped. No sense in getting Mom all mad when she could take care of it herself.

Day Two in the Garden…

Jason planted his potatoes today, but a couple of the pieces didn't have "eyes." Mom said he couldn't plant them, because they'd probably rot underground (that's where potatoes grow), but said twenty plants should be enough. Mom planted beets and corn. She found a lizard egg and gave it to Jason (against my advice) who said he had to help it hatch. She said he was going to bring the baby back because lizards were good for the garden and welcome to stay. I planted my carrots today and it was easy. All I had to do was draw one long line in the dirt with my finger instead of making a thousand holes. The soft dirt made it even easier. The real fun comes when I get to cut their "hair." Can't wait!

4

SOIL'S ALIVE

Jason rubbed a stripe of inky dirt beneath each of his eyes, then grabbed his football and wound up for a pass. "Nathan!" he shouted. "Go long!"

Jason threw the ball with all his might, hooting with delight when Nathan caught the spiral square in the chest. "Good catch!"

"Great throw!" Nathan yelled over his shoulder as he ran for a touchdown near the edge of the garden. He sailed past neatly tilled beds of black soil and leaped high over an imaginary goal line, but landed short, burying himself knee-deep in

soft soil.

Jason hooted with laughter. "Nice one!"

Nathan looked down at his jeans. "Aw, *man*! My mom's gonna freak when she sees me!"

Jason jogged over and checked out the situation. Black dirt was ground into Nathan's pants and seemed to fill his shoes. It wasn't anything they couldn't fix. "Tell her you fell," he said. "She can't be mad at you if it was an accident."

"I hope you're right," Nathan replied.

"Boys?" Jason's mom called from the house.

The boys turned toward her voice.

"Have you finished planting your beans?"

They were supposed to be planting Jason's red beans, but Nathan sidetracked him with a toss of the football. Jason surveyed the huge dent that Nathan's landing had forged in their line of dirt and shouted back, "Almost!"

Nathan gaped at him in disbelief.

"Okay. Lunch is in fifteen minutes!"

"We better fix this before she sees it!" Jason exclaimed.

Nathan hastily brushed the mess from his pant legs and the boys went to work. Scooping handfuls of dirt, they piled it back into place, patting it down as best they could, then scraped their fingers across the top, mimicking the action of a rake.

"Make sure it's really smooth," Jason said. This was his mother's corn row. If they messed up her seeds, she would not be happy. Glimpsing movement farther down the bed of dirt, he stopped and crawled over. "Hey, look at this," he said, and pulled a wriggly worm free.

Nathan brightened. "Live bait! Do you think there are any more?"

"Probably. Let's check!"

Jason and Nathan tore through the row, sifting dirt, crumbling it through their fingers as they scanned its contents. When they came up empty, they cast it aside and hurried on to the next clump.

"I found one!" Nathan exclaimed.

"Awesome." Jason expanded his hunt farther down the row, tunneling deeper into the neatly combed bed as he searched.

"Boys?"

They froze.

Jason's mom stood over them with hands on her hips. "What are you doing?"

"Uh, we—" Jason scrambled to his feet.

Nathan did the same.

Heart pounding, Jason lied, "We were—um—trying to fix this row of dirt." He pointed to the mess they'd made.

Nathan flashed a look of, is-that-the-best-you-could-come-up-with?

Jason's mom crossed her arms over her chest and the headlights of interrogation beamed bright. "And what were you shoving into your pockets?"

Jason gulped. "Well, we—um—found a couple of worms," he said, "and decided to save them for later. For fishing," he added, though it was pretty obvious. He was allowed to fish, right?

"But our garden needs worms, honey."

Jason frowned. She *wanted* the worms? He'd expected his mom to yell at him and Nathan for making a mess of their row, not be mad because they were taking worms out of the garden.

Nathan looked as confused as Jason felt. "But, Mrs. Williams, why would a garden need worms?"

"For food, Nathan."

Nathan gawked at her. "Food?"

"Yes, food." She smiled. "Much like you boys need a healthy diet to grow big and strong, plants need soil rich in organic nutrients so that they can grow big and strong."

"*Organic?*" Nathan asked. He glanced at Jason who shrugged. "What's that mean?"

"It means all natural," Jason told him. "We don't use any chemicals or toxins or stuff."

"That's right," Mom said. "And that's why we need worms."

Nathan looked like he was about to be sick. "*Plants eat worms?*"

"Nope. Even better." Jason's mom crouched down beside them and sifted through a handful of soil. "Worms live in the soil and eat the nutrients they find there. Then they poop."

The boys giggled.

"I know it sounds funny, but worm poop is one of the *best* types of food for plants. It's an excellent source of nitrogen.

Nitrogen is important because it helps the plants grow nice green leaves. With the help of the sun, big green leaves allow plants to make their own food. The process is called photosynthesis."

"Wow..." Nathan pulled the worm from his pocket, particles of dirt tumbling out with it. "I never knew that. I thought they were only good for fishing."

"Plants also need phosphorous and potassium."

"What are those?"

"Nutrients."

"She means food," Jason pitched in.

"Yes. Nutrients. Plants need them to grow, same as you boys."

Jason shrugged his shoulders. He didn't really care what plants ate, though the conversation was making him hungry.

Mom smiled. "Cow poop is also good for plants."

"Gross..." Nathan crinkled his nose.

"You feed them cow poop?"

She nodded and waved a hand over the bed of dirt beside him. "In fact, this dirt here is mostly cow poop."

Jason and Nathan exchanged a horrified look. They'd just been digging through cow poop!

"Don't be so squeamish, boys," she said. "A little cow poop never hurt anyone." She brushed the dirt off her hands and rose. "Finish up here, you two, then come in for lunch."

As his mom turned and walked away, Jason pointed at Nathan's dirt-covered pants and snickered, "Ha! You've got poop on your pants!"

"And, Jason," his mom said, turning back to them. "Be sure to wash your face." She winked. "You don't want to get any poop germs in your eyes."

Nathan pointed at Jason's face. "Ha, ha! You have poop on your face! Poop on your face! That's way worse than having poop on your pants!"

Jason scowled. "Whatever, poop pants."

"Poop face!"

Day 4 in the Garden…

P.S. Nathan Jenkins smashed into one of the rows while going out for a pass and then we found worms. Mom says they're good for plants but their poop is gross.

5

SLIPS OF MYSTERY

Lexi held the Mason jar with both hands as she walked along the edge of the garden. Jason passed, bumping her as he did so. Water spilled onto her hand. "Hey— watch what you're doing! You almost spilled my sweet potato slip."

He dropped his gaze to the hairy-sprouted orange potato overflowing from her jar. "Did not."

"Did so," she said, staring down his back as he turned down his bean row. Reason number three hundred and twenty-five not to like brothers: *They're totally insensitive.* Judging her potato sprouts to be

tely in one piece, Lexi carefully continued on her way over to Mom.

Mom looked up from her work with
the tomatoes and smiled. "Sweet potatoes
go in the last row." She pointed to the far
end of the garden. "Over there."

"Jason ran into me and almost *spilled*
my slip." The one she had painstakingly
pricked with toothpicks, suspended in water and diligently watched over until it
sprouted. Three long weeks. At this rate,
she might miss the deadline for the garden
contest! Staring down at the tangle of
white roots and green leaves, she felt a
rush of relief. But finally it had. This one
potato was going to produce a ton more.

About to walk away, Lexi noticed eggshells scattered across the ground near the
base of Mom's tomato plants. "What are
you doing with those?"

"Enriching the soil with calcium."

"Seriously?"

"Yes. Remember last year, how some of our tomatoes had ugly black holes in them?"

"Yes, they were gross. But what do eggshells have to do with it?"

"The marks were from blossom-end rot. It's due to a lack of calcium. This year I hope to change all that by adding egg-shells." She smiled. "They're an excellent source of calcium."

"Could you give them milk?" Lexi asked. "It's a good source of calcium, too."

"Sure is," Mom said. "And I probably could, but by adding the eggshells to the soil early on, I hope to avoid problems later. Remember: an ounce of prevention is worth a pound of cure."

Uh-oh. Mom was quoting old sayings again. Lexi's ears closed as she heard a lecture coming on, certain something about cleaning her room would be next, and hastily departed to do her potato work. Mindful not to spill any more water, she carried her sweet potato slip to the last row, away from all the other plants, and thought, *poor sweet potato, banished to the last row, left to grow all alone.* It didn't seem fair.

Except for the fact that sweet potatoes took up a *ton* of space. Like watermelons, their vines needed room to spread and they didn't stop for anything, not even other plants! Visions of last year's marigolds filled her mind—cute little yellow flowers Mom planted around the border of the garden and swallowed up after a week's vacation. They were covered by a carpet of dark green vines, greedy green vines from yours truly, the sweet potato. Lexi shook the thought away. No sense in pining over last year's loss, though she did love those flowers, especially drawing them. But now it was time to plant new flowers, new vegetables—like her sweet potatoes.

Setting the jars on the ground, she created a small hole, plucked off a green leafy sprout from the side of her sweet potato and gently placed it into the ground. Careful to keep the green "shoots" of leaves above the dirt, she lightly padded the dirt around the baby plant's base. Moving on, she pulled another clump of sprouts free from its hold of the sweet potato and wondered why anyone called them "slips" instead of sprouts. *How did that make sense?*

She delicately placed the plant into the shallow hole, and covered the stringy roots with dirt. That's what they were, sprouts from a half-potato piece. At least "shoot" described what the sprout was doing—shooting up and out from the potato. Though it seemed simple enough to just say sprout. Why make up a whole new word?

Lexi thought about that for a minute. Maybe it was because farmers were bored. They spent so much time out in the fields, they probably started making things up for the fun of it! She would, if she were stuck out in the garden all day long, nothing to do but plant seeds and slips.

"Hey, Mom!" Jason shouted. "I think we have a problem."

Lexi flipped her face up to see what he was talking about.

"What kind of problem?" Mom asked.

"Come look."

Mom rose and walked over to where Jason crouched between rows. He pointed to something on the ground near his bean plants. "Look at that."

Mom bent over for a closer look. "Oh, no...that isn't good."

Lexi stopped patting dirt around her sprout and called out, "What?"

"We have a visitor," Mom announced.

"Do you think it's Boomer?" Jason asked.

"No. This isn't the work of a dog. But I think I know why he's been barking at night."

"Why?"

She smiled at Jason. "You're the poop expert. You tell me."

Poop expert? Lexi got up and walked over to see what the heck they were talking about.

And she found it. There in the center of the walkway was a pile of poop. But not your average pile of poop. This one had strange things in it. Like seeds and berry-like pellets. "Gross."

"Does Boomer normally eat seeds?" Mom asked.

Jason thought about that for a moment. "Maybe he ate some fruit."

Mom shook her head. "I think we might have a raccoon."

Jason looked at her. "A raccoon?"

"What would they be doing in our garden?" Lexi asked.

"Well, they eat plants, fruits, insects, frogs—all kinds of things."

Jason stood, his brow creasing in concentration. "But how can you be sure it's a raccoon and not something else?"

"Jason's right," Mom said. "This requires further investigation to be certain." She walked around the area, searching for who knows what as Lexi and Jason followed. "Be careful not to touch the poop," Mom warned. "Raccoon feces can contain bacteria harmful to humans."

Lexi gaped. *Touch it?* Was her mother crazy? *She wasn't going anywhere near it!*

Mom continued her circular stroll around the garden, then pointed. "There." She bent over. "Do you see?"

"See what?" Jason asked.

"Paw prints."

Jason was on the ground in seconds, crawling around on all fours as he checked the dirt for animal tracks.

"Do you see them?"

He nodded and his eyes lit up. "Cool."

Lexi eased her head forward, but refused to get any closer. "But how can you be sure they're from a raccoon? It could still be a dog."

"Look closer," Mom said. "Notice how long the prints are in shape? Dogs have a more rounded paw."

Jason brushed some stray mulch aside to get a better look at them. "They look like hand prints. Hey—is that pointy tip from a claw?"

Mom leaned in and saw the scrape mark. "Looks like it to me." She patted his back. "Good job, Jason. Excellent detective work!"

Lexi did not like the sound of wild animals running through the garden. She

ventured a peek toward the house, toward her bedroom window. What if they made their way up there and clawed at her bedroom window? She shuddered at the thought. There was *no* way she was going to bed at night knowing a raccoon was on the loose. "How do we get rid of it?"

Mom straightened. "Good question." Tapping a finger to her mouth, she said, "It might be tough." She moved about the garden. Everything was sprouting, from beets to tomatoes, carrots to potatoes. It was like a buffet of fresh food—heaven for any hungry animal!

"Unless we plan to fence the garden, there's really no way to prevent them from roaming around out here at night," Mom said.

"They come out here at night?" Lexi asked, her worst nightmare confirmed. "But how can they see?"

"Raccoons are nocturnal, which means

they're most active at night. Their eyes are specially equipped for the darkness."

Jason leaped to his feet. "They have night vision!"

"Yes, much like possums and bears."

"Cool," Jason said.

Possums and bears? Lexi scanned the trees behind their home. What else was roaming around out here she didn't know about? Visions of wild animals jumping out from the woods burst into her imagination. "Mom—can I go to the house?"

Surprised by the abrupt change in subject, Mom asked, "Are you finished with your slips?"

"Yes," Lexi blurted, not sure if she was or not, but she didn't care. She had to get out of here!

"Did you check on your carrots?"

"Not yet." She glared at the poop on the ground. What if that raccoon pooped near the carrots? How would she be able to give her sprouts a haircut?

"Check on them and then you can go on up." Mom turned to Jason. "Guess that leaves you and me on poop-dispatch duty."

"Awesome!"

Lexi hurried over to her baby carrot sprouts, and race-walked past them. Yep, everything looked good. She grabbed her empty jar and jogged up to the house while Mom and Jason went hunting for poop.

Day 21 in the Garden...

My sweet potato slip was finally ready to go into the garden and I planted the sprouts today. Jason found a pile of animal poop, and we think it was made from a raccoon. We also learned that tomatoes need calcium, just like kids. Mom said next time we could experiment and feed the plants milk instead of eggshells. If it works, might be cool to tell the kids at school.

6

WACKY WEEDS

Jason slumped against the kitchen counter. "But why do *I* have to feed them?"

"Because Lexi fed them yesterday," Mom said as she cut tomatoes for her salad.

"But that stuff stinks!" *Literally*, like dead fish.

"Don't worry. You don't have to use the fish emulsion today. Try the blood meal."

"Blood meal? It sounds more like bat food than plant food."

Mom laughed and crinkled her nose. "It does, doesn't it?"

Timmy bounded into the kitchen, his hands marked with crayon. Eyes rounding, he asked, "Did someone say bat food?"

"We're talking about blood meal, not bat food. Blood meal is just like it sounds—blood—dried up and made into a powder. The plants love it because it's full of nitrogen and helps make them grow lush and green."

"Oh," Timmy said.

Jason's focus settled on his younger brother. "How come he doesn't have to feed them?"

"Because he's five and too young to manage the fertilizer."

"I'm only ten!" Jason protested, amazed by his willingness to revert to "little kid" status. Usually he was insulted if someone dared thought him to be younger than he was, but if it meant getting out of garden chores, well then, sure—whatever it took! He wanted to play

soccer today, not garden. "How hard is it to scatter plant food? It's easy. You scoop and scrape. Done."

Mom paused for a moment and seemed to consider his argument.

Intrigued, Jason stood by, silent.

Mom tapped her fingers against pursed lips. "Hmmm. Maybe he could help you with the weeding..." Spotting the mess on Timmy's hands, she pulled him over to the sink for a wash down.

Timmy looked up between the two of them as his hands were scrubbed clean. "I can weed!"

Jason couldn't believe his ears. Mom was willing to put the little guy to work? "Really?"

"Yes. I think it's about time he gets acquainted with the garden, don't you? After all," she added with a smile, drying Timmy's hands with a kitchen cloth, "he enjoys the harvest, too. Makes sense he should take part every step of the way." Letting go of Timmy, Mom wiped the over-spray of water from the counter.

It's past *time if you ask me,* Jason thought. Especially when it came to weeding.

"C'mon, Timmy. Let's go."

"To the garden?" His brother jumped with excitement. "Okay, let's go!" He scurried out the door after his older brother then stopped short and whirled. "I need tools. Where are the tools?"

Jason held up his hands and wriggled his fingers. "Here are your tools, all ten of them."

Timmy frowned. "Those aren't tools. I want real ones."

"Why don't you give him a hand tiller?" Mom suggested. "I think he can handle it."

Jason grunted and pushed his brother toward the door. "Fine."

Once in the garden, Jason turned to Timmy and said, "All right, here's the deal. You like to play swords with me, right?"

Timmy nodded.

"Good." Jason suppressed a grin. "Then we're going to play another game—kinda like swords only different."

Hand tiller in hand, a three-pronged rake-shaped weeding tool, Timmy nodded, intent on receiving his orders.

"I now pronounce you 'Weed Warrior,'" Jason said, flaunting an air of authority as he tapped Timmy's head. "You are a spy for the castle. Your mission, if you choose to accept it, is to be on the look-out for weeds." Jason brought a hand to his brow and pretended to be on the look-out. "They could be anywhere. On the walkway, in the row—even hiding behind the leaves of the plants. Your job is to grab them, pull them out, and toss them as far from the garden as you can!"

"Got it!" Timmy whipped around, ready to pounce, but stopped. His enthusiasm dimmed as he turned back to Jason. "What are weeds?"

Jason shook his head. *Kids.* They need everything spelled out for them. He walked over to Mom's row of beets and pointed to a clump near the base of their red stems. "Weeds are the little green plants growing in between the vegetables. The green stuff that *isn't* supposed to be in the garden. These are beets." Jason held a ruffly leaf with a red stem for Timmy to see. "They're good. These are weeds." He tugged at a patch of oval-shaped green leaves. "They're bad. Your job is to get them, pull them out, and throw them into that corner pile." He hitched his thumb in the direction of the fence. "That one, over there."

Timmy spied the pile in question. "Okay. Got it."

Jason went to pick up the bag of plant food while Timmy ran down the row. Reaching down, he clawed at the first sprouts he found and yanked them with his hand. Unfortunately, they were young potato plants.

"No!" Jason dropped the bag and raced over, grabbing Timmy's arm before he could do any more damage. "Not *those*—these." He directed him to the smaller, wispy sprouts. "See?" he asked, and yanked a bunch out. "Weeds." And why was the kid in this row, anyway? Beets, he showed him, beets! Not potatoes. Those were too valuable for a newbie to be messing with.

Timmy nodded vigorously. "Okay, got it. These," he repeated, and dove into action. He pulled and tugged and yanked until all the green leaves broke free, taking half the dirt with them. Moving on to the next group, he pulled and tugged and yanked with the same force, this time taking a few potato leaves with him.

Jason watched his brother at work and realized this delegating business wasn't going to be as easy as he first thought. Left alone, Timmy could pull out the entire row of potato plants, and no potatoes meant no contest money. It was unacceptable.

"Timmy." Jason sighed. "Stop."

Timmy stopped.

"How about you come help me with the food?"

Timmy jumped to his feet and charged him, tool thrust out in front of him like a lance. "Okay!"

Jason dodged the tool in Timmy's hand and grabbed the bag of blood meal. He scooped out some of the black powder and scattered it around the base of a plant. "I'll drop the food, you rake it in, like this," he said, and took the hand tiller from Timmy and scraped the soil where he'd deposited the fertilizer. "See? Easy."

"Got it." Timmy took the tiller from Jason and sat poised on his haunches.

Jason sprinkled. Timmy raked. Jason sprinkled. Timmy raked.

Well, this *is productive,* Jason groaned inwardly. If he didn't have money involved, he'd let Timmy do both. But if his weeding skills were like his feeding skills, there was no way Jason could chance it. "Grab that weed," Jason directed, and pointed to a stray grass-like tuft.

Timmy did as he was told.

Jason sprinkled some more fertilizer onto the ground and Timmy worked it in. "Now grab that weed."

Timmy responded. Things progressed well—under close supervision—until it was time to water. Jason filled the watering can and then lugged it between the rows, Timmy close at his heel—or so he thought.

As he bent over to water his row of beans, Jason caught sight of Timmy poking his nose into a bush at the opposite end of the bed. His brother started picking at something. Never a good sign.

"What are you doing?" Jason asked and dumped the last of his water onto the plants. When Timmy didn't respond, Jason walked over to him. Timmy began digging deeper into the leaves.

What the heck was he doing? "Leave the plant alone, Timmy."

"But there's a worm. See?" He pointed into the leaves of the plant. "Right there!"

Jason neared the bush and noticed that many of the bean leaves were curled over at the edges. "What the—?"

Timmy proudly opened his hand and revealed the gunk of a squashed green and yellow caterpillar. "See?"

Jason dropped the watering can to the

ground. "Aw, man!"

"I found it hidden in the leaves!"

Great. *Hunter boy was on the prowl.* Jason grabbed hold of Timmy's wrist to make sure he didn't smear the nasty goop on his shirt. Last thing he needed was Timmy wiping mashed caterpillar all over his clothes. Mom would kill him for letting that happen!

After a quick peek into the bean bush, Jason realized there were several caterpillars hidden among the leaves, wrapped up in some kind of cobweb. What were they doing—building cocoons or something? Flipping through stems, he realized many of the leaves were half-eaten. Jason groaned loudly. Just what he needed, a pest trying to eat his prize money. "C'mon, we have to wash your hands," Jason said, and pulled Timmy toward the hose.

"But there are more worms!"

"Not for you, there aren't," he replied with disgust. "What were you thinking smashing that caterpillar like that?"

Timmy made a serious face and said, "Bugs are *bad* for the plants. I was helping to get rid of them."

Jason couldn't argue with him there. "Yes, but you don't want to *wear* them, you want to *remove* them."

"I did!"

Timmy's face was so proud, his lack of guilt so genuine, Jason thought, *What's a brother to do?* He couldn't fault the kid for trying, could he?

Nah. At least he was having fun. "No problem, kid." Jason rumpled his hair. "Getting dirty is part of gardening. Next time, we have to get you dressed for the job, that's all."

Timmy paused, then his eyes lit up. "Can I get a 'Weed Warrior' costume?"

Jason laughed. "Why not?" Then brilliance struck. If Timmy learned to love the garden now, maybe he'd love it even more next year. And if he loved it more next year, then he wouldn't mind doing all the garden chores. Genius! "C'mon, Timmy—let's go see if we can't make you a costume!"

7

FEATHERY TIPS

As Jason walked toward the hose, dread seized him cold. Lexi and her friend Amy Watkins were barreling down toward the garden in their bathing suits. What the—?

If Lexi saw dead caterpillar on Timmy's hands, she would for sure tell Mom. Jason grabbed his brother's hand and sprayed water all over it. "Hurry—we need to clean this mess before Lexi sees it!"

"Jason!" The girls tumbled to a halt at the edge of the garden. "Amy and I are here to water the garden," she announced breathlessly. "Mom says you and Timmy

can go back into the house."

Jason pulled the hose from Timmy's hands. Was this a joke? "But Mom said I had to water all the plants after I fed them."

Lexi pondered that for a minute as she looked at the plants. "Did you?"

"I fed them, but only watered my beans so far."

A smile crossed her lips. "Well, you don't have to anymore," she declared. "Amy and I will finish the watering."

Jason didn't have to be asked twice. Joke or no joke, he was outta here!

Giving his brother's hands another look, he deemed all evidence of smashed caterpillar had been rinsed clean. Dropping the hose, he clapped a hand to Timmy's shoulder. "C'mon, buddy. We're off duty."

When she was sure the boys couldn't hear her, Lexi grabbed hold of the hose and squeezed the handle. "Water fight!" Amy shrieked.

Lexi began squirting water as Amy raced down the rows, hands flying in the air like she was running for her life. "Make sure you don't step on any plants!" Lexi warned, sending another gush of water overhead. "Those are our tickets to the festival!"

Now *this* was gardening. When she and Amy had been on their way to the pool, Mom asked if Lexi had trimmed her carrots. Suited up for a swim, she was horrified that her mother would bring up the garden at the worst possible moment. She had a friend over—this was no time for garden chores. Then Mom suggested they water the garden while they were there, too. Hot and dry, the plants were wilting.

Lexi's life had been ruined. Until her bestest-smartest-friend-in-the-world Amy asked, "Can we wear our suits?"

Unbelievably, Mom said okay!

And away they went. After all, Lexi had never met a hose she didn't like and chores-in-suits beat chores-in-shorts any day of the week! Treating her pal to another downpour, she decided this was WAY better than the pool. Not to mention they were being productive. Plants didn't care if the water they received bounced off the bodies of two crazy fun-loving girls, did they?

No way! Lexi squirted again and yelled, "Run, Amy! Run!"

When the plants were soaked and Amy out of breath, Lexi turned off the water. Tired after playing with the hose, she stared at the row of feathery carrots and frowned. Time for chores.

"So where are the carrots?" Amy asked, squeezing water from her ponytail.

"Over there, near the beets."

"How do we thin them?"

"We give them a haircut."

Amy's eyes widened. "Really?"

"Uh-huh." Lexi wanted the garden to sound exciting so Amy wouldn't tell everyone at school how boring her house was. "We get scissors and cut the sprouts."

"Can I try?"

Amy had uttered the magic words. "Sure. I'll go get the scissors!"

Racing over to the garden shed, Lexi returned and walked to the third row. With her chest heaving, she inspected two lines of feathery green leaves. The greens were teeny-tiny and as expected, crowded too close together. Setting hands to her hips, she looked at Amy with her most serious face. "These are carrots."

Amy followed her gaze. "They look like ferns."

"Those are their leaves."

"They don't look like leaves."

"Well, they are," Lexi replied.

She realized most kids didn't know what carrot leaves looked like. Last year, she brought her garden carrots to school in her lunch bag and all the kids were amazed by the fluffy greens attached to their ends and asked, *What are those?*

Obviously, they'd never seen home-grown carrots before. But being the expert that she was, Lexi took the time to explain to them that carrots had leaves when they came out of the ground. She even let them hold them. Her *friends*, anyway. Not those icky boys. Never know where *their* hands had been.

"Oh..." Amy replied, fascinated with the idea of cutting the carrots.

"Because the seeds are so small, they end up too close together. Now that they're beginning to grow, we need to thin them out and give them space or they won't grow big and fat." They'd end up skinny and scraggly and totally lose the contest for sure. "I'll show you how to do it," Lexi told her friend, "and then you can try."

Amy nodded eagerly.

Lexi kneeled down onto the ground and brought herself eye-level with her sprouts. At least this was a fun job. Aiming scissor tips between a heavy cluster of green sprouts, she clipped at their base with a steady hand. Pulling the fallen stems from between the others, she moved on down the row. "See how I'm giving them room to grow? Leave the biggest and cut the shortest."

"Gotcha." Taking the scissors from her, Amy bent down and peered at the greens. Sticking the scissors between them, she asked, "Is this good?"

Inspecting the bunch she was about to cut, Lexi determined it would be okay. "Yes. They need about an inch between them," she said, and held her fingers an

inch apart for Amy to see.

Amy cut, then carefully removed the greens as she'd watched Lexi do. Exhaling the breath she'd been holding, Amy asked, "Can I do another?"

Lexi couldn't believe it. Amy acted almost scared to cut them, but excited at the same time. "Sure."

Amy knelt and clipped, knelt and clipped. Before Lexi knew it, the whole row had been trimmed! Amy stood and handed over the clippers. "Thanks for letting me cut the carrots. That was fun!"

"No problem," Lexi replied, hoping Amy would tell everyone at school how much fun it was at Lexi Williams' house. "Now we have to put the greens on the compost pile."

"Compost pile?"

Lexi grinned. Amy looked like she was about to see a hidden treasure! "C'mon. I'll show you."

Day 33 in the Garden…

Timmy thinks weeding is fun because Jason told him he was some kind of superhero or something. Now he wants to make a costume and do it every day. (Kinda smart, but I'm not telling Jason.) They also found caterpillars folded up in Jason's bean leaves. Timmy squashed a couple, which is sad, because now they can't turn into butterflies. Maybe next time they should just MOVE the caterpillars from the garden instead of kill them. Amy Atkins came over and we played with the hose in the garden. I showed her how to give the carrots a haircut, and now she thinks gardening is fun and wants to come over and help every day! She'll probably tell everyone at school, too. She's the best friend ever, and I can't wait until we go to the festival together.

P.S. Mom says the plants are "progressing well."

8

SHINY FROGS & FLITTERING FLIES

Lexi folded her tiny dolly into a sitting position and gently placed her between the top stems of the potato plant. She locked one of the doll's plastic arms around a separate stem to fix her in place so she wouldn't fall out. Satisfied "Sally" was safe, Lexi sat back on her heels to admire her handiwork. Beneath Sally were "Suzy" and "Sarah," each snug within branches of the potato plant. Below them, Lexi had carved out a hole in the dirt, setting chairs and a beach ball around it. Peering at her configuration, she grinned. *Pool party!*

"You're supposed to be weeding."

Lexi jumped at the sound of Jason's voice. She whirled and saw him tossing a football up in the air, playing catch with himself. "I'm taking a break," she snapped.

"You're playing with your dolls. And what are you doing in *my* potato plants?"

Irritated with her brother's intrusion, she asked, "Since when is it against the law to play dolls in the plants? I'm not *breaking* any of them."

"They're my plants. Why don't you play with your own?"

"Because."

"Because why?"

They'd reached the inevitable standoff. She stared and he stared. Jason tossed the ball up, she watched it fall into his hands. Lexi knew he was waiting for her to give in but she would not. Reason number

eight hundred sixty-five: *Boys are nosy and pushy*. She refused to dignify his attack on her choices. She wasn't doing anything wrong. She wasn't hurting the plants. She was setting up a photo shoot for her dolls. Since when was it a problem to enjoy herself while working in the garden?

Jason strolled down the row next to her, as though reminding her he was still here. "Mom's right there in the garden shed."

"So." *Go ahead and tell her. I'm not doing anything wrong.*

Jason turned and walked away.

Lexi returned her attention to her dolls and screamed. "Ah!" Instinctively, she whacked a skinny black bug that crawled over one of her doll's shiny blonde hair.

Lexi's heart thumped hard against her ribs. Uh-oh. She got the bug, but she also broke one of the biggest branches on Jason's potato plant!

Jason ran back to her. "What happened?"

"There was a *bug* on my doll! And it was *gross*." She didn't even want to touch her doll—what if there were guts all over it?

"Did you break my plant?" Jason hollered.

Hearing the commotion, Mom hurried to the garden. Timmy followed close behind. "What's wrong? Are you okay?"

Lexi's heart skipped a beat. *Her dolls were in the potato plant! The broken branch!* "Nothing, nothing," she said quickly, moving her body in front of the dolls. Red-headed Suzy tumbled to the ground beside her, and fear sank to the pit of her stomach. There was no way to hide that—or the broken potato stem. It was split in half.

Lexi suddenly felt sick.

Mom walked up and looked at the

plants-turned-playhouse. She crossed her arms over her chest. Her gaze hardened.

Lexi's face turned hot. "There was a bug on my doll!" she screeched in protest. "It was crawling all over her!"

Mom nodded. "I see."

"I killed it," Lexi confessed.

Timmy's eyes grew wide. "You *killed* it?" His gaze darted to the plants behind her. "You killed a bug?"

Jason's interest perked. "There was a bug on my plant? Where?"

Mom frowned. "Did you think that was a good idea?"

"Uh..." Lexi paused, gripped by sudden doubt. Shouldn't Mom be glad she killed that bug? Weren't they always worried about insects in the garden? And Jason—it could have eaten his entire plant. He should be thanking her right now, right?

But neither of them looked happy.

Lexi gulped and ducked her head in reply. "Kinda."

"What did it look like?" Mom asked.

"It was long and skinny and *ugly*. Could probably eat a lot, too." Now Mom would understand that it had been the right thing to do.

"Hmmm..." Mom tapped a finger to her lips. "It could have been any one of a number of insects. What color was it?"

Was she crazy? It was the color of ugly! "What difference does it make what color it was? Big ugly insects aren't good for the garden."

"Unless they're beneficials."

"Beneficial?" Lexi fumbled through her memory of garden words. That meant *good*, right?

"Beneficials eat other insects that eat our plants," Mom said.

"Like the ladybug," Jason piped up. "They eat aphids." He turned to Lexi and

said, "Hey now, don't go killing any good bugs on my plants!"

Lexi glared at him. "Everyone knows that ladybugs are the good bugs because they're *girls*," she added, making sure her glare caught her brother square in the eye.

"Yes," Mom said. "But ladybugs aren't the only good bugs to have in the garden. Dragonflies are good to have around, too. Praying mantis, pirate bugs..."

Jason zeroed in. "Pirate bugs?"

"Pirate bugs?" Timmy repeated, looking from Jason to Mom and back again, equally intrigued by the sound of these menacing creatures.

"Yes, they're tiny bugs that feed on aphids, mites, even tiny caterpillars."

"That's disgusting," Lexi said and recoiled from the plant.

"Perhaps." Mom agreed. "But it is nature. Out in the wild, animals have to eat. That includes bugs."

"Cool," Jason said.

"Cool," repeated Timmy, alert to his brother's next move.

Lexi had no idea there were so many different kinds of revolting bugs out here. She whipped a glance toward her sweet potatoes. *Were they in danger of being attacked by bugs?*

"Lizards eat bugs."

"Yes. And frogs," Mom noted. "All these animals are helpful in the garden. They work within the cycle of nature, which is why we like to *keep* them around."

Lexi felt the ding.

"And don't worry, Lexi. While they like to eat bugs, flies and mosquitoes, they don't eat plastic."

Then they shouldn't be crawling all over my dolls! she wanted to shout, but only replied, "Good. Glad to hear it."

"By the way, are the girls enjoying their

nature adventure?" Mom asked.

Lexi eased into a smile. "Yes," she answered, adding a silent reply to her brother, *Told you I wasn't in trouble.*

Turning away, Mom said, "After you finish your weeding, Lexi, drop the broken branch off at the compost pile, will you? And try to be more careful next time. Jason's potato plant needs those branches to grow big, round potatoes." She reached out to take Timmy's hand, and the two returned to the garden shed.

"Hah!" Jason whispered once Mom was out of hearing range. "Play in your own plants!"

"Hah, yourself." She bobbed her head from side to side. "She wasn't mad."

"Was too."

"Was not."

"Kids," Mom called back over her shoulder. "*Trim* it!"

Both silenced on command.

Day 54 in the Garden...

Today I was playing in the garden with my dolls (which I've done a thousand times) and a bug crawled on them. It was SO gross. I killed it, and then Mom said I shouldn't have, because some bugs are good. I don't know how you can think any bug is really good. It's a bug! Timmy was happy to find bugs to kill, but Mom said it was better to spray the plants with a mix of dish soap and water. It traps the bugs and keeps Timmy's hands and clothes clean. Other than that, the garden is "progressing well" and almost ready for harvest (the fun part!).

9
POPPING PODS

Harvesting beans was not Jason's favorite job. There were too many of them, in too long a row. He didn't even like beans. Not anymore, anyway. Not if this is what it took to get them into his chili. Frustrated, Jason checked on his pal, Nathan. He was lying on his side a few feet away from him, propped up on an elbow. Even he was bored. Definitely not the play-over he expected.

Man—they should be playing soccer, football, anything but plucking beans!

"Our basket's almost full," Nathan said. "How many more does your mom

want?"

"All of them."

Nathan's expression dipped. "All of them?" His gaze ran the length of the bean row. "That'll take all day."

"Not really," Jason said, trying to inject some light into the depths of Choreville. "We're almost finished."

"Yeah, right."

Nathan was mad, Jason could feel it. All because *he* had entered a garden contest.

Dollar signs lit up in his mind followed by visions of the soccer shoes he wanted to buy. They would look so awesome on his feet, would make him run faster than anyone in school... But first, he needed to get these beans harvested or he wouldn't be able to win the money needed to buy the shoes.

Looking at Nathan, Jason felt torn. He wanted the money, but he wanted to hang out and play with Nathan, too. Jason turned back to his beans and thought, *maybe this garden contest was a mistake.*

Something hit his side. He turned to Nathan.

What the—? Did he throw a bean at me?

But Nathan seemed clueless. Busy pulling pods from the branches, he didn't even realize Jason was looking at him.

Hmph. Jason returned to the bush in front of him. Maybe Nathan was madder than he thought. Picking up his pace, Jason pulled three pods from the bush at one time, then popped the tan skins open, dumping the line of dark red beans into his basket, chucking the empty pods into another.

Another bean hit him, but this time it hit his knee. He whirled around and demanded, "Hey—what are you doing?"

Nathan looked up. His mouth dropped open. "What?"

"Why are you throwing beans at me?"

"I'm not." He reached into his bush. "I'm picking them, not throwing them."

"I saw you do it."

"No, you didn't." Nathan squared his shoulders. "I didn't do anything!"

"Better not do it again," Jason warned. Nobody threw beans at Jason Williams. Not even his best friend Nathan Lampert.

For the next several moments, the two continued their work in silence. Neither boy uttered a word, both intent on their business.

Pop!

This time Jason heard it *and* saw it. A bean spit itself clear out of its pod! Jason rose to his knees. "Hey, did you see that?"

Nathan looked over at him, mild curiosity cooling his anger. "See what?"

"A bean popped right out of its shell!"

"It did?" Nathan got up and came over. Squatting down next to Jason, he peered into the line of bushes. "Where?"

"Right there." Jason pointed at the twisted brown pod still attached to the bean plant by its stem then picked up the kidney-shaped bean. "This thing just shot right out of it!"

"Cool." Nathan searched the ground for others.

Jason held dark green leaves aside, and they spotted several beans lying around the base of the plants. "Look at all these! They must have popped out on their own because I didn't pick them. I swear."

"Whoa."

Jason picked one up. Across the garden, he spotted the metal frog his mom used to scare birds. Turning beneath the hook, its shiny surface reflected sunlight. Jason threw the bean at it.

Bing!

"Bull's eye!"

"Hey, let me try that," Nathan said. He

picked up one of the fallen beans from the ground. Jumping to his feet, he whipped it through the air.

Bing!

The smiley-faced frog spun wildly in reaction to each direct hit, flashing metallic rays of green.

"Way to go!" Jason cheered.

Nathan beamed. "This is fun!" He picked up another and sent it flying with a flick of his wrist. It missed.

Leaping up, Jason called, "My turn." Winging his bean through the air, his second shot was no better than Nathan's.

"Mom isn't going to like it when she hears you two are throwing her beans through the garden."

Jason froze. *Lexi.* He turned in place to find his sister standing behind them, camera in hand.

"And it's all documented," she said, tapping the edge of her camera, blue eyes gleaming with delight. "Right here."

Nathan stood by, horrified.

Jason wanted to tackle his sister. Take her to the ground and snatch that annoying camera clear out of her grip. "It's no big deal," he said, trying to sound convincing and unafraid. "It was only a couple of beans."

"A couple too many," she mocked.

Just then, Jason spotted Mom and Timmy walking out the patio door. *Crud.* Mom was already upset with him over his lost library book. Misplaced, to be exact. He didn't lose things, he misplaced them. For a *while.*

Jason's mind whirred at top speed. He watched Timmy run down the hill. Watched Mom cruise down behind him. They'd be here in less than a minute.

He turned to Nathan, who turned to him, his expression one of complete despair. Jason turned back to Lexi. "I'll clean

your room for a week if you don't tell Mom," Jason rattled off, hoping the promise would save his skin.

Lexi cocked her head to one side, her ponytail swinging along with it. "And do my breakfast dishes?"

Jason growled. "*For a week?*"

"Jason!" Timmy bellowed his name, running to the garden full sprint.

Lexi flicked a look toward Mom and said, "She won't be happy, you know. You're already in trouble for that lost book."

"Fine," he muttered. "I'll clean your room *and* do your dishes for a week. Now, do we have a deal?"

Lexi only smiled.

"Do we?" Jason demanded.

As Mom neared, Nathan whispered loudly, "Hurry!"

"Deal," Lexi said.

Timmy made a beeline for Jason but

stopped short. Distracted by something in the garden, he detoured down the broccoli row.

"How are you boys coming along?" Mom asked when she reached them. "Making good progress?"

Nathan gulped.

Jason cleared his throat. "Fine, Mom."

Lexi smirked and pranced off with her camera.

Mom walked over and checked the baskets. "My, you boys have been busy!" She set hands to her hips. "Didn't I tell you it would be easy, Nathan?"

"Yes, ma'am," he replied, then shared a guilty glance with Jason.

"Mommy, look!" Timmy called out. "A butterfly!" He followed the butterfly as it darted about the plants.

"Wonderful!" she called back.

"Hey, Mom," Jason said, confident he was in the clear, now that Lexi was gone.

"Did you know that beans popped out of their pods all by themselves?"

Pleased by his question, she said, "I sure did. It's how they replant themselves."

"We saw it happen."

"You did?" She clasped her hands together and looked from boy to boy. "That's exciting! I've never actually seen it happen myself."

"Happened more than once," Jason said, a new authority on the subject. "Here, I'll show you." He indicated for her to follow his lead as he bent down and pointed. "See this brown twisted pod? The bean popped out, right here. Look at the ground. You can see other ones that popped out, too."

Mom leaned in for a closer look. "Isn't nature amazing? Beans can grow all by themselves, without the skilled hand of a gardener."

Duh. Plants grew before people were alive. He'd learned that in first grade. "So, if beans can grow all by themselves, why do we have to work so hard to help them?" *Especially when we could be playing*, he thought, watching Timmy with more than a little envy. All the kid had to do was chase butterflies.

"Well, for starters," Mom began, "our yard is not the natural habitat for beans. Take these kidney beans. Many believe they were first discovered in Peru."

"Peru? Where is that?" Jason asked.

"It's in South America."

"How did they get here?" Nathan asked.

Pursing her lips, she thought for a moment. "Well, in many ways. Early explorers brought them to Europe, traded them with early settlers...Native Americans carried them across the countryside."

"Whoa," Nathan said. "Like on horse-

back?"

"Perhaps. It's also possible birds carried them as they migrated north."

Jason peered at her. "Birds?"

"Yes," she replied. "Maybe other animals, too. And once discovered, they spread quickly across the land as people learned to cultivate them and share them with others. It's how many of our vegetables came to this country."

A few feet away, Timmy tried to clap a butterfly between his hands.

"What does 'cultivate' mean?" Nathan asked.

"It means to work the ground," Jason said. "We dig up the dirt in our garden and make it loose so plants can grow better."

"How do you know that?" Nathan asked.

Jason shrugged his shoulders, but pride surged warm in his chest. "I don't know. I just do. I know a lot of stuff."

"Huh." Nathan's shoulders sagged. He shoved his hands into his front pockets. "I don't know anything about plants."

"Jason learned a lot of what he knows by working here in the garden," Mom said. "About insects, too."

Jason snapped to attention. *Someone mentioned insects?* He smacked Nathan on the arm. "Hey, you wanna go find lizards?"

Nathan sparked with excitement. "Sure!"

Timmy raced over and tugged at Jason's shirt. "Me too! Me too!"

"Have you forgotten the beans?" Mom asked. "There's still plenty left to be picked."

Jason glanced at his beans. *"Please,* Mom? We can finish up the beans later, promise."

"Well, you did make some great progress... Maybe a break would be good for you."

Better than good—it would be great! Jason hit his friend on the arm. "C'mon, Nate—let's go!"

"Take your brother with you!" Mom called after them.

Day 75 in the Garden...

Jason and Nathan actually saw beans pop right out of their pods today! Mom said it was normal because that's how they grow in nature. They have habitats and grow where the dirt and water is just right (like Goldilocks!). In our garden, we have to try and give them the perfect amount of water and food to grow.

Except in our compost pile. Everything grows well in the compost pile. Last year we had squash, tomatoes and *potatoes trying to grow in the pile all by themselves which must mean it's the perfect vegetable garden habitat. I took pictures of everything so I could show Amy.*

P.S. Mom said Jason didn't have to wait until his beans popped out of their pods. He could have picked them when they were "green" and let them dry off the plant. I think he prefers the dried beans, hint, hint. They're more fun.

10

BUGS, TUNES & COBS

After breakfast, Lexi and her friend, Amy, headed to the garden. They'd just had the best sleepover ever and now it was time to harvest carrots. Amy couldn't wait. Ever since the day she'd helped trim the carrots, she'd acted as if they were part hers. Which was totally fine with Lexi. She loved that Amy loved the garden. Besides, they both had a stake in the outcome. Free tickets to the Fall Festival!

And judging was in three days. Three days! Lexi giggled. She could almost smell the kettle corn and pumpkin pie, the sweet scent of hay and the stinky odor of horses. It was her favorite event of the year! But first, they had to harvest the carrots.

"C'mon!" Lexi shouted. Unable to control her excitement, she took off running. "Let's harvest some carrots!"

"Right behind you!" Amy yelled.

In seconds, the two of them were standing at the end of the carrot row. Thick lush greens burst from the ground in a perfectly formed line. Thanks to a steady finger, Lexi's bed of carrots was picture perfect. She'd taken numerous pictures to prove it.

"What do we do?" Amy asked.

"It's easy. All we have to do is loosen the dirt around each carrot and then pull it out."

"That's it?" Amy asked, her mouth agape.

"That's it!" Lexi squealed and dropped

to her knees. "I'll show you." When Amy dropped to a squat next to her, Lexi started digging the dirt around the base of a carrot.

"Don't we need gloves?" Amy asked.

Lexi stopped sudden. "I totally forgot!" Dipping into the basket where she had placed the gloves, she slipped a pair on and indicated Amy should do the same. "Okay," she said, and poked her fingers around the carrot. "Find a carrot and run your fingers around it, like you're digging."

Amy did as told, going after a carrot in front of her. "Like this?"

Lexi checked her technique. She was stabbing her gloved fingers deep into the soil around the carrot. "Perfect. You're already an expert!"

Amy giggled. "You think so?"

"Yep. Now, wiggle the carrot back and forth until its roots loosen."

"Roots? Carrots have roots?"

"Sure. All plants have roots," Lexi said. "Except these roots we eat."

Lexi pushed her carrot to and fro in the dirt until she felt it give. Then loosening the dirt a little more deeply, she pulled it free. Brushing dirt from its length, she declared, "Ta-da!"

Amy's breath caught and she stared. "Wow, it's so big."

"Thanks to your great haircut!"

Amy looked at Lexi. In seconds, her face turned from shock to pride. "I did that, didn't I?"

"You sure did." Lexi dropped her glance to the bed of dirt and carrots. "Pull yours free."

"Okay." Amy wiggled and waggled then pulled her carrot from the ground. Like Lexi's, it was long and fat with a few stringy pieces hanging from it. Lexi pointed at them. "Those are its roots."

"Really?"

"Yep. It's a root, but it also has little roots that grow from it."

"How do you get them off?"

"Break them off," she said, and ran a gloved hand up and down the carrot until the stringy pieces fell away.

Amy looked from carrot to bed of carrots, back to the one in her hand. "That's so cool. Let's see how many more we can get!"

"Let's do it!" Lexi agreed happily and dug in.

Half an hour later, Mom, Jason, and Timmy strolled down to the garden. "How's it going, girls?"

"Awesome," Lexi replied. She waved a hand over their basket. It was overflowing with long, fat, beautiful carrots.

"Gorgeous!" Mom exclaimed.

Jason gaped. "You got all those from

your row?"

"Yes, sir."

Timmy squatted and plucked one from the basket. He tried to stick it in his mouth, but Mom pulled it free before he could take a bite. "Let's wash that first, honey. There's still dirt on it."

Timmy looked up at her as if she were crazy. Lexi grinned. Because she and Amy had done an excellent job of wiping them clean.

"I want one," Jason said.

"Go ahead," Lexi offered. "We have plenty!"

Amy grinned. "Like hundreds!"

Well, that was stretching it, Lexi thought but didn't care. Amy could brag all she wanted. This was part her harvest, too!

"Would you girls like to help us harvest the corn?"

Lexi blinked. "The corn is ready?"

"I believe so. That's what we came

down to check."

Lexi flipped her gaze to Amy. "Wanna help?"

"Absolutely!"

The girls leaped up and ran to the row of skinny corn plants, their leaves flapping lightly in the wind like a hound dog's ears.

Jason ran over and wrapped his hand around one of the plump cobs. Timmy joined him and grabbed a cob, same as his older brother. "I wanna help!"

"Timmy, no!" Lexi exclaimed. "You'll break it!"

Jason screwed his expression. "You're supposed to break it. How else are you going to get it off?"

"Kids," Mom called out and walked over. "Hold on. We need to be sure the cobs are ready before we harvest them."

"How can you tell?" Jason asked, his hand still on his cob. "It feels ready."

Mom smiled. Leaning between the

children, she pointed to the strands of silky hair sticking out from the end of the cob. "When the corn silk is brown, the cob inside has likely matured."

"Matured?" Jason asked.

"Grown up," Lexi said. Something her brother had yet to do. Grabbing a cob with crispy brown hair, she pulled.

"Whoa," Mom said. Reaching over to help, she said, "We twist, not pull. Like this, see?"

Together Mom and Lexi grabbed hold of the cob by its base near the stalk as the others looked on. With their opposite hands, they held the stalk steady. "One, two, three!" Mom called out and with a slight tug, they twisted it away from the plant.

"Wow," Lexi said. "That was easy."

"I wanna try one!" Jason said, but released the one in his hand. The hairs were still delicate and golden-green. Moving to a plump husk farther down the plant, he twisted and pulled. "Cool!"

Mom laughed. "Harvesting is one of the best jobs in the garden. It means it's time to eat!"

"Can I try?" Amy asked.

"You bet." Mom looked at the plants and suggested, "Why don't you try this one?"

Amy went to the corn plant and placed a hand on the cob. "This one?"

"That one looks good."

Amy held the center stalk of the corn plant, held the cob and twisted with a quick yank. "I did it!"

"That you did," Mom agreed. "Why, if I didn't know any better, I'd think you had your very own garden at home."

"What about this one, Mom?" Lexi touched a huge cob near the base of another plant. "How long before this one is ready?"

"When the first strands poke free," she replied, "begin counting days. When about twelve to eighteen have passed, check them again. If their silk is brown and dry and they feel full and plump, you can pick them!"

"I call dibs!" Lexi told Jason.

"That's not fair!"

"Is too!"

"Is not!"

"Kids," Mom intervened. "There are enough cobs for everyone, okay?"

Timmy ripped the pale green husk from the cob his mother had given him.

"No, Timmy. Not yet. We want to refrigerate them before we cook them for dinner tonight."

He frowned.

"Maybe we should have waited until just before dinner," Lexi noted.

"Actually, we pick corn in the morning, before the sun has had a chance to warm it up. That's when it's sweetest." She winked. "And we like our corn sweet, don't we?"

"Sweet!" Timmy repeated.

Day 99 (or 3 months and 1 week) in the Garden...

Today was really fun. We got to harvest our first carrots and corn! Amy helped. The carrots were easy. We just dug them up and brushed them off. The corn was really cool. Hold, twist, and pull—even Timmy got to do it. Mom told us the secret to knowing when to pick is to count days. I'm saving some of the husks so that Amy and I can make some corn husk dolls. We're having a barbecue tomorrow to celebrate the harvest.

I can't wait! So far, our vegetables look pretty good. I hope they win! (My fingers are crossed.)

11

SWIMMIN' & BUZZIN'

Mom knelt before the bed of potato plants and slipped on her gloves. "Now that our plants have died back, we can begin to harvest the potatoes. Afterward, we'll do the same to Lexi's sweet potatoes."

"Do I have to wear gloves?" Jason complained, holding the pair of gloves in the air like they were poison. "They look dorky."

"When swimming for potatoes, you don't want to get dirt under your fingernails. What if you run into a grub and mush it?"

"Ee-yoo." Lexi grimaced and glared at her mother. "There are bugs in that dirt?"

Mom shrugged. "Could be. You never know, which is why you have to be prepared."

Ugh, Lexi thought, and reluctantly pulled on her gloves. Digging for potatoes was like digging for buried treasure. She hadn't even thought about bugs! Eyeing the ground, Lexi frowned. Mushy ones, at that.

"Okay. Remember, potatoes grow *under* the plants, so we have to gently loosen the soil around their base as we use our fingers to dig for potatoes."

"Why can't we use a shovel?" Lexi asked. "Wouldn't that be easier?" *And our hands wouldn't have to touch grubby, mushy bugs.*

"We don't want to use shovels because the sharp edge will scrape open the delicate skin of our potatoes. We want to cure them for better storage. We can't do that if they've been cut."

"Cure them? But they're not sick, are they?" Lexi looked at the potato plants. Actually, they did look kind of sick and wilted, their leaves all dead and brown.

Mom laughed. "Cure means drying. We dry the potatoes and toughen their skin for better storage." She winked. "That way, we don't have to eat them all in one day."

"Hey, Mom," Jason called out. "Look!"

Lexi and Mom both turned. Jason had left their side and wandered to the broccoli. He pointed to a broccoli plant on the end. No longer dark green, it was now bursting with yellow bloom.

"Yes, I know," Mom said. "With the recent warming spell, it's gone to flower. We didn't get to it in time."

"No," he said. "I mean the bee."

"Bee?"

Lexi and Mom walked over to Jason. Sure enough, there was a large bee hovering above the yellow broccoli flowers.

"Do you know what that is?"

Staring at the enormous bee, Mom asked, "Is this a trick question?" She looked from Lexi to Jason. "It's a bee, right?"

"It's a drone bee."

"Really?" Mom asked, but it didn't sound like she believed him.

"Sounds like someone is watching too much *Star Wars*," Lexi muttered.

Mom chuckled.

Jason ignored them both. He *knew* what he was talking about. "He's the defender."

"The defender?" Mom asked. "Wow... I didn't know they had *defender* bees."

Lexi gaped. "Are you making this up?"

Jason explained, "He's not a worker

bee. Actually, his job is to protect the queen bee."

"You mean, sort of like Dad does for Mom," Lexi replied.

He nodded.

"But what about the other two?" They were much smaller than the larger one. "Are they worker bees?"

Moving in for closer look, he nodded and pointed. "See how they fly into the flower? They're collecting pollen so they can spread it around. I remember this from third grade." He smiled. "That was over a *year* ago, and I still remember it!"

"See," Mom told him. "That means you *learned* it. And that's great!"

"We should take a picture!" Lexi exclaimed.

"You bet," Mom said. "Pictures of garden life are fun, but be careful. You don't want to get stung."

"I will." Lexi hurried to the house to

grab her camera, passing Dad and Timmy as they made their way out to the garden. Jason's friend, Nathan, was with them.

"Hey, Nathan," Jason yelled. "Come see this bee!"

Nathan took off running for the garden.

Timmy scrambled from his father's arms. "Bee! Bee!" Dad set him down on the ground, and he raced over behind Nathan. "I want to see the bee!"

"Be careful," Dad cautioned, following him to join the others.

As everyone huddled around the broccoli plant, Nathan asked, "Where's the bee?"

"There," Jason said proudly, pointing at the hovering insect as it darted in and out of the yellow flowers.

Nathan's eyes widened. "Cool."

Timmy tried to touch it, but Dad held him back by the shoulders. "Look with your eyes, not with your hands," he told him.

"Whoa…" Timmy uttered.

"Did you know that bees can visit fifty to a hundred flowers during one collection trip?" Mom asked.

"No way!" Jason exclaimed.

She nodded. "And they make more than one trip every day."

"That's why they're called worker bees," Jason said. "These guys work *hard*."

"Actually, worker bees are girls," Mom corrected.

Nathan and Jason gaped. "Girls?"

She nodded.

Lexi arrived with her camera and started taking pictures. "I'm going to show everyone at school! We have our own bees!"

Dad laughed. "Maybe we should start our own backyard bee hive."

Lexi pulled the camera from her face.

"We can have our own hive?"

"Why not? We could construct a simple hive and encourage the bees to visit your garden."

"You know," Mom brought a gloved finger to her mouth. "That's not a bad idea. Without them, we don't eat. They work to pollinate our flowers and vegetables."

"Pollinate means to help flowers grow," Lexi said. "I learned that in science class."

"Yes. Pollen is the fertilizer for flowers. Many of our fruits and vegetables start as flowers before becoming the parts we eat." Placing hands to hips, Mom asked, "Should we get back to the business of swimming for potatoes?"

Nathan looked around the garden. "Swimming for potatoes? They grow in water?"

"It's just a figure of speech," Mom

said. "We call it 'swimming for potatoes' because digging through the dirt with your hands is like swimming through water."

His eyes lit up. "Can I try?"

"Sure. Let's all have a turn!"

Returning to the row of potato plants, the kids watched as Jason's mom showed them how to dig around under the plant. Now that Nathan was wearing a blue pair of gloves that looked exactly like his, Jason didn't feel so weird. Even Dad wore them!

Running his fingers deep in the soft dirt, Jason hit something. "Hey—I think I found something!" It was small and round and yanking it free, he brushed the dirt from the red skin. Excitement pounded in his chest. "It's a potato!"

"Oh, that's a big one," Mom said. "The perfect size for French fries!"

Jason burst into a smile, one that took up his whole face. "Or potato chips!"

Nathan popped up from the hole he was digging with one of his own. "Look at this one!" He held it close to Jason's and compared finds. "It's huge!"

"Not as big as mine," Jason replied.

"They both look big to me," Jason's dad said.

"I say we make potato chips *and* French fries," Mom exclaimed happily. "We have enough for both."

From farther down the row, Lexi pulled up a smaller potato. "Is this too small?" she asked.

Mom shook her head. "Not for potato salad, it's not!"

Dad rose from his knees. "I say we make it a party. Anyone up for a barbecue on the grill?"

"Can I invite Amy?" Lexi asked.

"You bet," Mom said. "It's fun to share the harvest! The more the merrier."

"But you can't eat all my potatoes," Jason warned. "I need some for the contest. Like this one." He whipped his hand behind his back. "We can't cook it until the judges see it."

Mom smiled. "Agreed."

Later that afternoon, seated at the picnic table, Lexi showed Amy how to tie the waistband for their corn husk doll's skirt. Using twine, they each made a big bow.

"Look, Mom!" Lexi held her doll up and pushed the long stringy hair down behind her back.

"Look at mine!" Amy said, walking her doll across the tabletop. "She's a model corn husk doll."

Mom had surprised the girls by showing them how to add long hair to their dolls' heads. A total improvement, considering the ones they'd made earlier in the day were bald.

"I love it!" Mom exclaimed. "Very nice

work."

Lexi's doll was a brunette, because she had used brown corn silk while Amy had a blonde.

"Can we paint eyes on their faces?" Amy asked.

"You can do whatever you'd like," Mom said. "Only your imagination is the limit. But you might have better luck with a marker." She turned to Lexi. "Why don't you run get some from the office?"

Lexi jumped up from the table. Her mom kept a whole pack of colors on her desk, which was usually totally off-limits. "I'll be right back!"

Jason watched his sister run to the house and briefly wondered what she was up to—until Dad called him back to their project. "We can build our bee-hive box with these simple instructions."

"Can I use the saw?" Jason asked.

"After a lesson, you bet. We'll use it to-

gether."

"I can help," Nathan pitched in. "I helped my dad build a birdhouse once."

"Excellent," Dad replied. "Building projects always work better when we have more hands to help."

"We'll have to be sure we follow all the safety rules with the bee-hive," Mom said. Standing by the grill, she was turning the corn cobs.

Jason's stomach grumbled. The sight of grilling burgers and corn on the cob made him hungry. "Can we start tomorrow?" he asked.

"Tomorrow is the Farmer's Market contest judging," Mom said.

Jason was so excited about their new building project, he totally forgot. Whipping his head toward Nathan, he said, "We can't miss that!"

Day 106 in the Garden...

Today we got to swim for potatoes. It's kind of a weird way to think about digging through dirt, but we had fun. Right in the middle, Jason found a bee flying around my broccoli. Some of them were covered in flowers, and the bee was there to get their pollen. Or nectar. I'm not sure which. Mom said we could build a bee-hive for them. Kinda cool...except that bees make me nervous. I'm also nervous about the contest tomorrow. We're supposed to bring our vegetables in for judging, and I hope we win. Amy and Nathan want to go. They're thinking they might want to enter next year! They came over for dinner and Mom made healthy French fries with Jason's potatoes which were yum. Amy and I made corn husk dolls. Funny, that the "trash" from the corn cobs can be put to good use.

P.S. Fingers crossed for tomorrow!

12

JITTERY NERVES & COLORFUL SWIRLS

Lexi and Jason fidgeted as they waited. Their basket of produce was set out on a table before them. Jason had brought his potatoes and beans. Lexi brought her carrots and sweet potatoes. They also brought their friends, Nathan and Amy. It was judgment day. The day they learned who won and who lost.

"I want a fruit slush!" Timmy whined.

"Not yet, sweetheart," Mom said quietly. "The judges are almost here."

Lexi grunted. *Not fast enough, they were-*

n't. The judges were strolling around the tables at a snail's pace, oohing and aahing over every fruit and vegetable they saw. What was taking so long?

"I don't think they're going to like ours," Jason said. "They're not nearly as big as some of the others."

Lexi scowled. Reason number seven hundred and thirty-two not to like brothers: *They're downers.* "Bigger doesn't always mean better, ya know."

"Does so," he replied.

"Does not!"

"Kids," Dad said. "No arguing."

"Dad's right," Mom agreed. "There's no need to fuss." She placed a hand to Jason's shoulder. "And Lexi's right, too. Bigger isn't always better when it comes to fruits and vegetables."

Jason's brow rose. "It isn't?"

"No. Quality is what counts when it comes to the food we eat." Reaching between them, she pulled one of Lexi's carrots from the basket. "Look at the shape of this carrot. It's perfectly full and tapered toward the end. And the color," she added, pausing as she turned it to and fro. "It's the most beautiful shade of orange I've ever seen."

Lexi stood a little straighter on her chair. "See." She jutted her chin. "My carrots can definitely win."

Mom smiled. "They sure can." Then she picked up one of Jason's potatoes and said, "Your potatoes, too."

Jason stared at it, then swiped a glance over his shoulder to the table next to them. "Yeah, but theirs are twice as big."

"They're also a different variety."

Jason lifted his brow. "Huh?"

"Not all potatoes are created equally. Yours are 'new potatoes' and meant to be smaller." She winked. "Makes them more tender and delicious."

"Well, no matter what the judges say," Dad offered, "I think your vegetables are out of this world, and you two did it all by yourselves. You should be proud."

"Me, too!" Timmy whirled around and exclaimed, "I helped!"

Dad laughed, and Mom replied, "You sure did. As did Amy and Nathan."

Amy and Nathan exchanged an uncertain glance.

"Everyone be quiet," Lexi hissed. "They're coming!"

Amy and Nathan hovered in the background, their eyes growing large and round as the judges neared.

An older man approached their table. Pinned to his shirt was a huge blue name tag that read: JUDGE. Slowing, he looked at their vegetables, then he looked at them, then back to their vegetables.

Lexi gulped. Was that a bad sign? Or were they so beautiful, he couldn't keep

his eyes off them?

"Hello," Mom said.

The judge lifted his head to face her. "Good morning."

No smile. The man had no smile! Lexi whipped a glance to her brother. Did he see it, too? The gloomy look in his eyes said, *yes*. Lexi dropped her gaze to the vegetables on the table. She couldn't bear to face her friend, Amy. If they didn't win, she wouldn't get free tickets to the Fall Festival. Amy might decide to go with Kimberly Evans instead. Lexi wanted to burst into tears. It wasn't fair!

"Are these your carrots, young lady?"

Lexi looked up at him. "Yes," she squeaked.

He picked up one of her carrots and turned it over in his hands, running his fingers down one end and up the other. Then he brought it to his nose, closed his eyes and sniffed. Lexi pulled back in her

seat. *He wanted to smell it?*

Jason's eyebrows shot up in surprise. Mom and Dad said nothing. Timmy reached for a carrot and Lexi slapped his hand flat to the table. He probably wanted to smell a carrot, too, but he wasn't allowed. Only judges.

Opening his eyes, the judge smiled. "This is amazing."

Lexi blinked. Amazing? A carrot? She thought it a bit weird, but since he sounded happy, she wasn't about to say anything to change his mind. Amy elbowed Lexi from behind, but Lexi was afraid to look back.

Next, the man touched their beans and potatoes, sniffing and running his hands over them, too. Lexi thought he looked like he wanted to take a bite out of one.

"Our vegetables are completely organic," Mom said, as though it would make a difference.

Lines formed across his forehead as he paused. "Really?"

"Yes, sir. The children and I insist on growing only vegetables that are safe to eat."

"You know," he said, glancing from side-to-side as though sharing a secret, "I wish all vegetables were grown organically. It would make my job of judging a pleasure."

"How so?" Dad asked.

Again, looking around for anyone who might overhear, the judge hushed his tone as he said, "Gardening is about the land, being outdoors. It's about living in tune with nature. These days, people have become so used to fast food and brightly-colored packaging that they forget what real, wholesome food is all about." Glancing between Lexi and Jason, he continued, "Getting kids involved in growing their own food is so important. It teaches them where food comes from and how to appreciate it." Suddenly, his mouth tightened into a hard line. "My grandchildren think every meal should come with a prize."

"Well, it's not a bad idea," Jason said. At the judge's displeasure, he quickly added, "But I'd much rather eat French fries made from my own potatoes! They taste *way* better."

"I'm sure they do," the man said.

"Would you like to try a sample of our potato salad?" Mom asked, pulling a container from a cooler located beneath their table.

The judge's eyes widened as she opened the container before him. Mom handed him a plastic fork. He cleared his throat and replied, "Well—er—don't mind if I do."

He ate the first bite, and once again his eyes closed, then rolled beneath his lids like he was having a wonderful dream.

Chewing as is if it were the first bite of food he'd had in a week, the judge groaned. Lexi crossed her fingers. It sounded like he liked it. Looking to their mom, the judge said, "Oh my, those potatoes melt in the mouth like butter!"

"Thank you," she replied.

"I think all organically grown vegetables taste better," he said. "There's less water and waste and more of what you're after—flavor."

"I agree," Mom said. "Would you like another bite?"

Glancing in both directions, he lowered his voice and said, "I'd love to, but I really shouldn't. You know, I wouldn't want anyone to think you're bribing me."

Bribe away, Lexi thought, feeling the first tingles of excitement. *Whatever it takes to win!*

Mom smiled. "I understand."

The judge sighed. Picking up a potato,

he commented, "This is beautiful, and the perfect size for a serving of salad."

"Would you like to take it with you?" Mom offered.

Lexi whirled. Why was she giving their vegetables away? That was no way to win a contest. And if she was going to give anything away, give him the carrot. He'd already put his nose all over it.

Suddenly, a woman judge appeared at the table beside him. Peering down at the vegetables now spread out across the table, she didn't seem as impressed. Lexi's heart caught. Would she vote against them?

Like the first judge, she picked up one of the carrots. Inspecting its size, she asked, "Did you not have enough time to grow them?"

Lexi stared. What was she talking about? They started the minute they saw the poster advertising the contest! Lexi opened her mouth to tell her exactly that when the first judge nudged the carrot toward the second judge's nose. "Take a smell."

About to object, the woman did as instructed and her eyes widened. She looked at him, then to Lexi and Jason, Mom and Dad. She smelled again and closed her eyes. "It's heavenly!"

Judge number one nodded with a small smile. "I thought you'd enjoy it."

Instantly, the woman began to pepper them with questions. What kind of carrot was it? Did they buy the seeds locally? Did they use special fertilizer?

As Mom answered the questions, Lexi stole a peek at the table next to them. The family of five was not happy to see *two* judges standing at the Williams' table when one should be moving on to *theirs*. Lexi erupted into a grin. Well, maybe they should have grown organic vegetables in-

stead of those gigantic zucchini and squash!

Maybe the judge was right. Maybe the big vegetables didn't taste as good as the small ones.

Filled with a growing sense of pride, Lexi eased back next to her friend, Amy. Maybe Mom *did* know best when it came to vegetables and gardening. A squiggle of thrill zipped up her spine. And maybe they could win!

Two hours later, the judges called everyone to the center of the Farmer's Market as they prepared to announce the winners. Lexi stepped forward with mixed feelings. On the one hand, two of the judges seemed to like the way their vegetables smelled. But three others stopped by and didn't say a single word, though one asked if they could take a sample carrot home with them, to which Mom, of course, said yes. Why did she continue to give all their stuff away? How about these people go home and grow their own vegetables?

Jason didn't seem to mind. He said Mom gave food away to lure the judges into voting for them, kinda like when you hook a worm. Give the fish a taste of the worm and he'll want to chomp down for the whole delicious thing. When he did—snag!—that's when you hooked him.

Lexi didn't know about all that. She only knew she wanted to win.

"Ladies and gentlemen, may I have your attention?" A hush settled over the crowd. "It's time to announce the winners for our First Annual Kids' Gardening Contest." Everyone cheered. Waiting until the noised quieted, the man continued, "First we'd like to thank everyone who participated. It was great to see all the wonderful homegrown vegetables and meet the children who grew them."

As the man droned on, Lexi mumbled under her breath, "Announce the winners already!"

Mom placed a hand to her arm. "He's getting there, sweetheart. Patience, patience."

Patience was for pond watching. She wanted to hear the winners!

"I bet you're going to win," Amy encouraged with a whisper.

Jason and Nathan stood by, quiet and completely still.

"And now for the moment you've all been waiting for... In third place we have the Davis family!"

Loud shouts and claps exploded as two girls marched up to the center stage area to collect their ribbons. Smiles and handshakes followed.

"Second place goes to the Miller family!" A group of people across the way roared, and Lexi covered her ears. Three boys elbowed their way forward and ran up to the man for their ribbons.

Sheesh. Who would have thought that a silly old ribbon would have gotten them so excited? But in that second, Lexi's heart pinched. If her name wasn't called next, she'd have nothing—no ribbon, no tickets, no nothing. As she watched the second place winners jog back into the crowd, her stomach filled with dread. Smiles were pasted on their faces as their parents received them with hugs and congratulations.

Jason began to squirm. "Hurry up!" he shouted under his breath.

Lexi didn't want to think about losing. She didn't want to think about how she would feel if they lost. Mom and Dad would pretend it was okay, but Lexi wouldn't be. And Jason wouldn't be. Lexi latched onto her brother, and the two shared an uncertain gaze.

They were a team, a unit. Their hopes hung on the same outcome. For the first time, Lexi felt scared for her brother. It was the same thing she felt for herself. Lexi crossed her fingers even harder. Jason noticed and did likewise.

"It was a difficult decision for the judges," the announcer said. "Everyone did an outstanding job, and we almost couldn't decide."

Heart pounding in her chest, Lexi held her breath.

"But after much discussion, we decided the winner of the First Annual Kids' Gardening Contest is...the Williams family!"

Lexi gasped, then shrieked at the top of her lungs. "We won!"

Jason pumped a fist into the air. "We did it! We won!"

Without thinking, Lexi grabbed hold of Jason and hugged him. "I won the tick-

ets!"

"I won the money!"

Mom and Dad laughed and said at once, "You did it!"

Timmy jumped up and down. "You did it! You did it!"

Realizing she was hugging her brother—her brother!—Lexi let go and cried, "I can't believe we won!" Turning to Amy, she squeezed her tight, jumping up and down. "We won! We won!"

Mom placed a hand to her back. "Go on up and claim your prize."

Releasing her friend, Lexi shook like a leaf. *They'd won.* Jason was already headed toward the judges, and Lexi quickly followed. Her legs felt so weak, she feared she might trip! But she managed to climb the stage and take up position next to her brother.

The two "sniffing" judges placed the ribbons and medals around her and Jason's necks and handed them the prizes. Jason took the check. Lexi took the tickets. Turning to the crowd, she looked for Amy and cheered. "We're going to the Fall Festival!"

Day 107 in the Garden…

We weren't actually in the garden today. We went to the Farmer's Market for contest judging and we won. WE WON! Now Amy and I can go to the festival and Jason has the money to buy his soccer shoes. I didn't want to say it out loud because I didn't want to jinx it, but when we arrived at the market and I saw all the other kids' vegetables, some were really huge, and I thought for sure we weren't going to win. I think Amy thought the same thing, but she didn't say anything. (She's too nice.) Then they called our name and it was the best day ever.

We won…I'm so happy! And next year, Amy says she definitely wants to have her own garden—if I promise to help her. I told her of course I'd help her. Gardening is WAY fun when you share it with friends. Much more fun than sharing it with your younger brother, though I have to admit, Jason did a great job. (I think it was his potatoes in the salad that won the judges over.)

P.S. Can't wait until next year!

P.P.S. I'll write all about the festival after Amy and I go.

THE END

VOCABULARY WORDS

Beneficials ~ Insects and bugs that are good for the garden, because they help remove the bad bugs from your plants.

Compost ~ Organic soil made from the breakdown of organic matter like kitchen scraps and discarded plants.

Crop rotation ~ The practice of changing a plant's location each season based on bugs and soil conditions. One way to remember is to sing: beans-leaves-roots-and-fruits!

Cultivate ~ The process of breaking up the soil surface (till), removing weeds, and preparing for planting.

Fertilizer ~ A word used to describe a food source for plants.

Harvest ~ The process of picking your fruits and vegetables when they are fully grown.

Nutrients ~ Vitamins and minerals plants use to grow like N-P-K (Nitrogen, Phosphorous, Potassium)

Organic ~ The method of gardening that uses only natural materials made from living things.

Pesticide ~ Something used to kill bugs and insects.

Photosynthesis ~ The internal process by which a plant turns sunlight into growing energy; the formation of carbohydrates in plants from water and carbon dioxide, by the action of sunlight on the Chlorophyll within the leaves.

Till ~ The process of loosening the soil to make a nice, soft bed for growing plants.

RECIPES

HEALTHY FRENCH FRIES

And I do mean healthy. Nothing sinister going on with these fries, only fresh wholesome goodness and the flavor of pure potatoes–sweet potatoes or white! Both work very well.

What you'll need:
several potatoes, sliced lengthwise and to the thickness of your liking

olive oil

spices — rosemary/garlic powder

Preheat oven to 375°F
Brush potatoes with olive oil and spices. An easy way to do this is by placing your oil and seasoned potatoes in a large plastic bag, sealing it closed, and then pressing

the fries around inside to thoroughly coat them. Rosemary and garlic powder are a GREAT combo for both sweet potato fries and regular white potato fries, but salt and pepper work well, too.

Arrange sliced potatoes on a cooking sheet in a single layer and bake for about 45 minutes. If you like your fries crispy, bake longer. For softer fries, bake for less time—you choose! But either way, these will be the BEST fries you ever tasted, especially if you grew them yourself!

FLUFFIEST CARROT CAKE

This carrot cake differs from most in that it's light, fluffy and kid-friendly—from the making to the eating! Not only can they help by harvesting and shredding the carrots, they'll love to decorate this spring treat (bunnies, anyone?). While this recipe calls for cream cheese frosting, a bit tangy for some youngsters, it would also be great with a creamy white/vanilla frosting, too.

What you'll need:

2 cups self-rising flour
2 tsp cinnamon
1 ½ cups vegetable oil
4 eggs
2 cups sugar

3 cups freshly grated carrots
½ cup raisins (optional)
½ cup walnuts, finely chopped (optional)
pre-made fondant for decorations

Preheat oven to 350°F

Grease or butter 9 x 13 or 2 8-inch round pans. In a large bowl, combine oil, eggs, and sugar and beat well. In a separate bowl, combine flour and cinnamon and mix together until creamy smooth. Add dry ingredients to wet and blend well. Fold in grated carrots, followed by any optional items of your liking!

Pour batter into pan and bake for about 35-45 minutes or until knife inserted into center comes out clean. Serve with cream cheese frosting (even plain, *this cake is so good*).

Approximately 1 large or 2 8-inch cakes.

CREAM CHEESE FROSTING

So easy to make, thick or thin—your choice!—and tastes great. It's the perfect addition for your carrot cake.

What you'll need:

8 oz. cream cheese, refrigerated

2 TBSP unsalted butter, softened (at room temperature)

1 ½ – 2 cups powdered sugar (depending on how thick you like your frosting!)

1 tsp vanilla extract

dash of grated orange zest (optional)

Combine cream cheese, butter and vanilla extract in bowl and blend until smooth. Add sugar gradually, 1/2 cup at a time, beating until blended. Stop when you have reached your desired consistency. For stiffer frosting, use more sugar. For creamy frosting, use less. Stir in optional flavorings at end. Spread (or drizzle) frosting over cake and enjoy!

Note: You can purchase packages of pre-made fondant at most major craft stores, and forming your figures is easy. We used a tube of green cake decorating color for the greens on our carrots—for a more feathery effect. Don't forget the pre-made flowers and sprinkles—talk about EASY—you'll have a stylin' cake in no time!

SWEET POTATO PIE

And I do mean sweet. This version of sweet potato pie is creamy and delicious, a sure winner with adults and kids alike. At our school garden, the kids went CRAZY for it!

What you'll need:
- 2 cups sweet potatoes, cooked
- 1/2 cup heavy whipping cream
- 2 eggs
- 3/4 cup sugar
- 1 tsp vanilla extract
- 1/2 tsp cinnamon
- 1/2 tsp ginger
- 1/4 tsp nutmeg
- pre-made pie crust (or make your own!)

whipped cream (optional but totally YUM)

Preheat oven to 350°F.

Pre-bake pie crust to near golden completion, but not completely. Set aside. In a large bowl, combine potatoes, cream, eggs, sugar, vanilla, and all spices and blend well. Blenders make this part easy and the result is oh-so-smooth and silky. Pour batter into awaiting pie crust and bake for 35-45 minutes. Time may vary, depending on your oven. When done, knife inserted should come out clean.

Place on rack to cool. This pie is best served warm, though allowing it to cool somewhat will make for easier slicing. Add a dollop of whipped cream and enjoy!

Recipe doubles well.

COMFORT
CHILI

This chili is simple and tasty. You can top it with all kinds of tasty things like cheddar cheese, sour cream, or chopped green onions. For those spicy ranchero types, add some chopped green chile peppers. *Yeehaw*, that chili bites back!

What you'll need:
- 1 pound lean ground beef
- 1 TBSP canola oil
- 1/2 cup chopped sweet onion
- 1 can (14.5 ounces) diced tomatoes
- 1 1/2 to 2 cups cooked kidney beans
- ½ teaspoon chili powder
- ¼ teaspoon paprika
- ¼ teaspoon cumin
- 1 teaspoon salt

½ teaspoon black pepper

Heat oil in skillet on medium-high heat. Add meat and chopped onion and cook until beef is browned. Add remaining ingredients. Cover and simmer for 20 minutes. Chili serves 6.

Note: If using fresh picked mature kidney beans from your garden, there's no need to soak overnight before cooking. All you have to do is put your beans in a pot of water, bring it to a boil, then reduce the heat to simmer and cook for about 30 minutes. This will soften the beans and make them ready to add to your recipe. However, if you allow your beans to harden (great for long term storage), then you'll want to soak them overnight to help soften the beans before cooking. Remember, the canned beans you buy at the store are very salty. If you like them salty, make sure to add a few teaspoons of salt to your pot of water when cooking your beans.

POTATO SALAD

Potato salad is a classic, sure to win over the fussiest of customers (even judges!). And better yet, you can change it up by adding your favorite ingredients.

What you'll need:
2 pounds red potatoes
3 hard-cooked eggs, chopped
¼ cup chopped bacon bits
½ cup mayonnaise
2 TBSP sour cream
1 TBSP spicy brown mustard (Dijon-style)
3 green onions, chopped (optional)
1 tsp salt
½ tsp pepper

Place potatoes a large saucepan and cover with water. Bring to a boil. Reduce heat and cook covered for 15-20 minutes, or until tender. Drain potatoes and quarter, then place in large bowl. Stir together potato and egg. Add bacon bits. Stir together mayonnaise and next 3 ingredients, then gently stir into potato mixture. Season with salt and pepper. Serve immediately, or cover and chill, if desired.

Makes 8 servings.

LESSONS

STARTING FROM SEED

Seeds are like babies. They need lots of care. Actually, lots of WATER—especially during the first few weeks. Seedlings need to be kept moist or they won't sprout. Moist means not too dry, not wet—kinda like Goldilocks!

How deep should you plant them? Look at your label, but tiny seeds (like carrots) must be planted 1/4" deep while larger ones (like beans) should be about 1" deep.

What kind of dirt is best for your seeds? Fine, loose dirt, that holds its moisture well. Moisture means wetness. But re-member Goldilocks—not too wet, not too dry. You can buy potting mix from the store. Unlike the dirt in your backyard, you can sure it's clean of disease so your young seedlings can stay healthy.

And we want them healthy so they can grow big and strong—just like you! Seeds also like to be kept warm. If they're not, they might take too long to germinate (a big word for sprout), *and that's not good.* Seeds need a quick and strong start on life—just like you need a strong and healthy start to the day! How do you start your day strong as a kid? *Eat a good breakfast.* How do you start life strong for a plant? Put them by a sunny window and they'll stay warm and happy.

What's another reason you want them by a sunny window? Without you to feed them, plants need to make their own food. But how?

Solar energy! In a process called photosynthesis, plants change solar energy (the sun) to chemical energy (sugar) with the help of carbon dioxide and water. In photosynthesis, solar energy is converted to chemical energy and stored in the form of glucose (sugar).

The chemical equation for this process is:

$$CO_2 + H_2O + sunlight = FOOD$$

But when you're there to help, give your seeds a little N-P-K. *Seeds love it.*

What is N-P-K? Simple! It's Nitrogen, phosphorous and potassium. Look for these letters on every bag of plant food and soon you'll get the hang of it.

N-P-K
nitrogen-phosphorous-potassium

Once your seeds sprout, keep an eye on them. Don't let them dry out, or get too hot or too cold. If you do, they'll stress out. This is sort of like "freak out"—only worse, because it will slow their root growth which is bad. Roots are the way plants gather their food from the dirt. It's how they stretch out and stand tall. When they're big enough, you'll want to transfer your seedlings to the garden, and if they don't have strong root growth, how will they take a firm root hold in the garden?

They won't. So take extra care with your seedlings and they'll take care of you with big healthy vegetables you can eat.

Now go get gardening!

ORGANIC MULCH BASICS

Mulch is a protective layer used on your soil to retain moisture, reduce erosion, prevent weed growth and best of all, *if it's organic mulch*, it will improve the condition of your soil, providing nutrients as the material decomposes. How great is that? But what is organic mulch, exactly? Where does one find it?

That's the best part. Organic mulch is all around you, from pine bark and needles to dead leaves and grass clippings, you already have a variety of mulch on hand. Even wood chips and shredded branches can be used. Shredded fall leaves are one of your plant's favorite mulches, but for strawberries and blueberries, go with the pine. It increases the acidic value of their soil and berries love acid. *Funny how they turn out so sweet.*

Caution on the grass clippings: make sure they are weed seed free else you introduce a slew of trouble into your garden. Weeds are amazingly agile and can grow anywhere—even on top of landscape paper!

And for you farm folks, grab a bale of hay or straw and spread it around your garden, on your rows and between your plants. While you're at it, check with Mabel the cow and see if she minds you borrowing some old poop of hers (old being the key word). Composting cow manure is a great source of organic mulch (and soil amendment) as well as a scoop from your kitchen compost pile!

No trees and no cows? No problem! Gather your old newspapers and some unbleached cardboard (think shipping boxes) for excellent weed prevention. You can layer whole sheets of newspaper or shred them, whichever you prefer. Cardboard is easily cut to size and blocks even the heartiest of weeds. Eventually they will both breakdown, but in the meantime, these two are winners.

Organic mulch will have to be replaced every year, but when you consider how valuable a resource it is for your soil, you'll be more than happy to oblige. Healthy soil is the first ingredient to healthy plants. *And the secret to easy maintenance.*

Sounds like a lot of work. Is it really necessary? Yes. Trust me, strolling through a weed-free garden admiring your plants is a heck of a lot more delightful than walking by weed after weed, nagging reminders of chores yet to be done. Your garden should be a place you WANT to spend your time, not a place you HAVE to spend your time.

At least for me. I have too many other things pulling at my attention to repeat tasks that shouldn't need repeating! Do it right the first time and layer it on thick and you'll be glad you did.

COMPANION PLANTING

Companion planting is the idea that certain plants benefit others when planted next to, or close to one another. One reason is pest control, naturally, without the need to use chemicals. In other words, plants have friends in the garden that help them. But they also have foes (plants that aren't good to have around them).

Rosemary repels cabbage moths and carrot flies, so plant rosemary near cabbage and carrot and they will be happy and pest-free! In the opposite way, the dill plant attracts hornworms. Hornworms love tomato plants so if you plant these two together, your tomato plant will not be happy—its leaves will be eaten up!

Other ways that companion planting can be beneficial is when it comes to nutrients.

Beans will fix nitrogen into the soil. Plant corn (heavy feeders) in the same bed next season and they will be happy.

The marigold flower, along with other plants, is well known for companion planting, because it exudes chemicals from its roots, especially helpful when it comes to nematodes. You can't see these pests, but they can see the marigold—and run! Whiteflies and other pests don't like the smell of the marigold flowers, protecting neighboring plants from the dreaded flies. But don't plant these flowers next to bean plants.

Companion planting also works in a physical way. Tall-growing, sun-loving plants may share space with lower-growing, shade-tolerant species, resulting in higher yields from the land. Not only does it use space better (more vegetables in less space), but it helps in other ways, too. Three sisters is the term which refers to planting corn, squash and beans together.

Squash provides ground shade to prevent weeds from growing. Corn provides the support for beans to climb. Beans provide extra nitrogen in the soil—for hungry corn and squash!

Other examples? Sunflowers and corn make good companions. Sunflower attracts the ants and aphids away from the corn and are also said to improve the flavor of the corn. Sunflowers are so tough, the ants and aphids don't bother them! To discourage raccoons from ravaging sweet corn and sunflower seeds, plant prickly vines around your corn and sunflowers.

There are lots of ways to use companion planting in the organic garden and good reasons, too. It helps avoid the use of chemical fertilizers and toxic pesticides. It also improves the quality of the soil.

So check your list of friends and foes before planting next season and you'll be happy, too!

FEED WHAT YOU GROW

What do your plants like to eat? N-P-K. Nitrogen-Phosphorous-Potassium. These are represented by the three numbers you see listed on the package of store bought fertilizer. 5-1-1 = 5 parts nitrogen, 1 part Phosphorous, 1 part Potassium (Example: This is what you'll see on the fish emulsion label.)

Like breakfast, lunch and dinner, these three basic nutrients are important. Like you, plants need food to help them grow big and strong. But same as kids, plants have likes and dislikes. Cabbage loves nitrogen, but not beans. They make their own. But where do we get nitrogen? Well, the rain for one. Ever thought about how after it storms, the plants and lawns look greener? It's because they get a "nitrogen kick" from Mother Nature. But if it doesn't rain, then what?

Try worm poop (everyone's favorite!), composted cow manure, blood meal, fish emulsion and the like. Stinky, icky, but delicious nitrogen sources for plants.

For phosphorous, give your plants bone meal and rock phosphate. And for potassium? Try seaweed extract and wood ashes.

Hm. Plants eat weird stuff. Now when you feed them, you need to mix it into the soil around the base of your plants. Like a "mini till," you work it in and water well. This way, it goes straight to the roots.

Perfect! And last but not least, a great soil amendment to continuously feed your plants is compost. By adding some of your outdoor pile of homegrown dirt to your plant beds, you're giving them a wonderful source of nutrients—even more than the N-P-K listed above.

SCENTSIBLE PEST CONTROL

Prevention is key when it comes to organic pest control. From plants to bugs, there are many ways to prevent bad bugs from invading your garden—but first you have to know the difference.

Who are some of the bad bugs?
aphids and beetles
caterpillars and hornworms
leaf hoppers and leaf miners
mosquitoes and moths
slugs and snails
squash bugs and whiteflies
grasshoppers and crickets

Which ones are good?
assassin bugs and pirate bugs
ladybugs and green lacewings
dragonflies, frogs and hoverflies
praying mantis and some wasps

Good bugs are also known as *beneficials* because they "benefit" your garden by keeping plants healthy and strong—and bug-free!

But don't forget the flowers. These can also be helpful because some bugs are "repelled" by certain scents so you'll want to be sure to include these in your garden. One of the all-around best is French marigold. Not only does it repel nematodes (microscopic bugs in the soil), it also discourages whiteflies, flea beetles and aphids. Geraniums repel red spider mites and horseradish repels potato bugs. Snails and slugs hate wormwood.

Speaking of "good scents," you can also use aromatic plants to prevent pests. Ants don't like peppermint and spearmint. Cabbage moths will steer clear from rosemary. (Hey, this reminds me of companion planting!) And the one plant that repels them all, including some kids? Garlic.

You can also use garlic to make a bug spray. Mix it with cloves and hot pepper and then watch out bugs—this yucky smelling spray is coming to a plant near you! Old coffee and water make a great spray, too.

Caution: wear gloves and don't touch your eyes before washing your hands.

You can also make a bug spray by mixing your compost with water. Let it sit for a few days and **presto** you have anti-bug spray! Yuck for you and yuck for bugs. And all your sprays will work a little better if you add a bit of dish soap to the mix— or combine it with water and use it on its own! Soapy water stops pests in their tracks.

Best way to stop the bugs? Use your "nose!"

CROP ROTATION

Organic gardening is an environment friendly and healthy way of gardening. It's also a way to garden in harmony with nature. Crop rotation is basically the planned order of crops planted in the same bed. It's a very important part of organic gardening, because it helps to prevent disease and replenishes the garden by putting nutrients back into the soil. Rotation of crops should be done each season.

When rotating crops, you don't want to plant the same family of plants in the same beds. Some insects and disease-causing organisms are host specific and will attack plants that are from the same family—the pests will be ready and waiting! Also, cucumbers leave toxins in the soil where they have been planted that can cause tomato plants to die. Corn uses a lot of nitrogen, so rotating with peas or beans will replenish the nitrogen back into the soil. And speaking of soil, rotating crops according to root systems will help aerate soil. Examples of vegetable groups and their rotation would be:

beans - leaves - roots – fruits
beans and peas (beans)
cabbage, broccoli, spinach (leaves)
carrots, onions, beets (roots)
squash, pumpkin, tomatoes (fruits)

light – heavy – light - heavy
Beans (light feeders)
leaves (heavy feeders)
roots (light feeders)
fruits (heavy feeders)

deep – shallow – deep - shallow
beans (deep roots)
leaves (shallow roots)
roots (deep roots)
fruits (shallow roots)

ABOUT THE AUTHOR

D.S. Venetta lives in Central Florida with her husband and two children and part-time Yellow Lab—Cody-boy! When not whacking away at her keyboard crafting her next novel or spending time with her kids, you'll find her in her organic garden chasing grasshoppers and plucking hornworms. When she's not knee-deep in dirt or her imagination, D.S. Venetta contributes gardening advice for various websites and schools. It's a busy life to be sure, but at the end of the day, if she can inspire someone to stop and smell the roses (or rosemary!) and be kind to Mother Earth, then she's done all right.

You can find her across social media:
twitter @DSVenetta
facebook.com/DSVenetta
pinterest.com/DSVenetta

Learn how to become a member of her fan club on her website, and be eligible for special discounts, advance excerpts, author swag, and unique gift items throughout the year. You can find all the information on her website: www.DSVenetta.com Then, sign up for her newsletter and be the "first to know" when her next book is released. You won't want to miss a single one!

D.S. Venetta hosts a garden blog where she makes gardening easy and fun! For more details: www.BloominThyme.com.

BEANS, GREENS & GRADES

Book #2
Wild Tales & Garden Thrills series

Lexi and Jason Williams take center stage at school when Principal Gordon enlists their help to establish a school garden at Beacon Academy. The kids are thrilled to be selected as Green Ambassadors for this important project, but quickly learn how challenging it can be to work with others toward a common goal. Not only must they teach their fellow students how to garden, Lexi and Jason feel the pressure to make it fun and exciting (or become known as "The Most Boring Gardeners Ever" in school history). When the principal reveals a generous amount of grant money has been offered to continue the green program if the children succeed, the stakes rise.

No worries! Lexi and Jason are up to the task, assisted by their student council members. But as they formulate, organize and implement the plan for Beacon Academy's first school garden, the kids are sidetracked by trouble, toils and trauma. Everyone has their OWN opinion on how to care for their plants, what should be done, and who should be doing it.

Hey—wait a minute. Who's in charge around here?

Find out in book 2 of the
Wild Tales & Garden Thrills series

Book #1 ~ Show Me the Green!
Book #2 ~ Beans, Greens & Grades
Book #3 will explore community and
library gardens ~ spring 2017

Coloring books available for each title featuring all of the illustrations from the book ~ perfect for engaging younger children in the adventure of gardening!

47395684R00160

Made in the USA
San Bernardino, CA
30 March 2017